Sliding

Sliding Doors

Peter Howitt

SCREENPRESS BOOKS

First published in 1998
by ScreenPress Books
28 Castle Street Eye Suffolk IP23 7AW

Photoset by Parker Typesetting Service, Leicester
Printed in England by Clays Ltd, St Ives plc

Photos by Alex Bailey
The Spanish Inquisition sketch used by permission of Python (Monty) Pictures Ltd

Peter Howitt is hereby identified as author
of this work in accordance with Section 77 of the Copyright,
Designs and Patents Act 1988

A CIP record for this book
is available from the British Library

ISBN 1 901680 13 4

For more information on forthcoming ScreenPress Books,
contact the publishers at:

ScreenPress Books
28 Castle Street
Eye Suffolk
IP23 7AW
or fax on: 01379 870 267

2 4 6 8 10 9 7 5 3 1

Contents

For my parents

John Hannah had been in our offices on the kind of general meeting often put together by agents in order to introduce actors to film-makers in Hollywood. He talked fondly but sadly about a film he was about to make but that had suddenly lost financing. He was clearly enthusiastic about the script and left it for us to read.

An enormous number of screenplays come to our production offices in California. They are almost always disappointments. The statistics are staggering. For good reason; writing a really good original screenplay is nearly impossible. I was only on page five of this one when I knew it was something we wanted to make at Mirage. Like many first-rate ideas, it seemed such an obvious premise that it was hard to believe no one had done it before. It took me about an hour to race through it and make the first phone call to try and raise the money to get it made. As it turned out, that was the only phone call I had to make. It was to Guy East at Intermedia Films in London and he was immediately interested and encouraging about the prospects, despite the fact that Peter Howitt was a brand new director.

Peter has written a screenplay that keeps one constantly guessing about how it's going to work itself out. There is genuine wit in the telling and a truth to its observations that makes one smile over and over. It never runs out of suspense or humor or fun, and manages to be touching by the time you reach the last page.

If you've seen the film, reading this screenplay will let you revisit these people and their foibles and their wit. If you haven't seen the film, I envy you the discovery of their world.

Sydney Pollack

When Peter Howitt first told me the idea for his debut feature film over dinner three years ago, my initial reaction was: 'What a fantastic idea', followed swiftly by 'How the hell could this idea be translated onto film?' Three years and numerous headaches and drafts later, I think we finally hit on the formula.

The draft published here is the fourteenth, but there were several 'unofficial' drafts in between, bringing the total number closer to twenty – unusual for a British film but vital in this instance. Before we became involved with Sydney Pollack and his production company, Mirage, Peter, myself and Doug McFerran (who as well as playing Russell in the film also acted as an excellent script editor in those early days) went through so many different scenarios for each 'story' that it would take too long to write them all down here. We finally came to the realisation that for this dual plot-line to work we had to strip it down to its most basic premise, which we decided was essentially a love story, and it all began to come together from that point on.

The making of this film in itself would make fascinating reading to any aspiring producers or directors, although unfortunately most of the really interesting things that happened while trying to raise the finance in the UK would be too libellous to print. Suffice it to say that Peter and I ended this experience on the one hand thrilled with the fact we had actually got the film made and on the other hand totally exhausted, although a good deal wiser. The way the film finally got made is the stuff I thought you only read about happening to other people: one grey cold afternoon I was sitting staring out of my office window contemplating the fact that our latest chunk of finance had fallen through again and wondering why I had ever decided to make films in the first place, when the phone rang. On the other end was somebody purporting to be Sydney Pollack asking if he could get involved in the film, as he had read it by chance that afternoon in his office in Los Angeles. Within a week our fairy godfather had secured the financing required to make *Sliding Doors*. Gwyneth Paltrow came on board soon after and the rest, as they say, is history.

The script itself makes an interesting study on structure and storytelling because of its complexity. Ultimately, the film is down to Peter Howitt's unfailing conviction in it and determination to see his first screenplay get made. I am delighted and proud to have played a part in its journey to the screen.

Philippa Braithwaite

Introduction

I had the idea for *Sliding Doors* walking down Charing Cross Road one day in 1992. I had a call I had to make to my then business partner John Flanagan. I couldn't decide whether to wait till I got home and make it or cross to the phone box on the other side of the road and get it out of the way. I flipped the cerebral coin of decision in the air and both options span around and around in the millisecond that these things do in our heads. It landed on the 'call him now' side. I walked out into the road without looking right left and right again and was nearly flattened by a car. The germ of the film came from that. What if I had been killed at that moment simply because of a phone call that could easily have waited? How different was my day going to be anyway because of that decision? I was already not experiencing the 'version' of me that carried on walking to the tube and went home to phone John. But does 'he' or any of his 'energy' still exist somewhere? I'll never know. You can't examine that syndrome in your conscious existence. But maybe you could in a film, I started to ponder. Can you tell a story that follows 'both' possible scenarios in one life at the same time? No idea. But it wouldn't leave my mind. For two years it kept knocking on my brain teasingly asking me when I was going to try and write it.

Eventually in June 1994 I gave in and started to type haphazardly, with no real idea of what I was doing. Of course the film's negative reviewers will suggest that that condition remained until the final cut!

Because of the rather whacky premise the film has I was never sure in the early stages whether it would actually be a worthwhile idea for a movie or end up being just an interesting thought that I should have allowed to slip from my mind. I wanted someone to tell me it was worth seeing through to the end of the first draft apart from my mum whose discerning 'Ooh, I like the sound of that' or 'No, I don't like the sound of that much' was my normal yardstick for continuance or abandonment.

So, I approached Philippa Braithwaite. Actually I approached Martin Clunes who I knew vaguely from the odd lovie booze up. I knew he was going out with Philippa and that she had produced *Staggered* that Martin had directed. We had dinner and I gave Philippa the first thirty pages of draft one and asked her to let me know if she thought it was shit or not. She called me a few days later and said she was fascinated by the concept and wanted me to finish it because she wondered how a premise like this would tie itself up at the end. She wasn't the only one!

Immediately after that in winter 1994, with half the first draft complete, I looked at my watch and realised it was time to have a major nervous breakdown. So I did. Funny things breakdowns, at the risk of sounding phraseologically oxymoronic. Everything stopped – eating, talking, walking, sleeping. The only two things I seemed to be able to do were cry and write. A strange combination which, working resolutely as a team, saw to it that by January 15 1995 I had a completed first draft of *Sliding Doors*, albeit considerably tear stained.

Philippa read the full thing, which in retrospect was a shocking tome, and liked it enough to embark foolishly on trying to help me get it made. We had no idea what an incredible journey it was going to be. It would lead us not only to condone the words of William Goldman when he said that in the film industry 'Nobody Knows Anything' but also wonder why so many of the people we were about to encounter pretended that they knew quite a lot!

It has to be remembered that in the jingoistic cinematic cycle of the Brits being in various stages of either 'Coming', 'Going', 'Thinking about coming back', 'A little bit lost on the M6 south of Droitwich', etc. that in spring of 1995 the British Film Industry was definitely in having a major heart surgery with lots of producorial surgeons looking at its valves and arteries and doing large head shaking intakes of breath.

We tried all the major accepted 'routes to finance' – you have to get that expression to trip off the tongue if you're going to make a movie. Channel 4, BBC Films, Granada Films, British Screen, Ken Branagh, er . . . oh, that's it. Or it just about was it in 1995. No Lottery then asking you to fill out seventy-eight forms and questionnaires.

At the same time as this Philippa had sent it to some distributors – those that also funded films – such as Fine Line, Miramax, Entertainment, etc. and a few established British production companies like Working Title. They all seemed to like it. Some of them loved it. People started calling me. 'I'm hearing amazing things about your script – can my mate at Blah Blah company have a look at it?' – 'Sure.' Polygram wanted to read it. It had become a 'hot' script. I got quite excited. Who am I kidding – I got fucking excited. I bought a new family size box of tissues – and I wasn't crying anymore!

Meetings were set up. C4 asked us to write another draft. 'This is such a good idea I'm not going to let you get away with this draft' were David Aukin's actual words. I wrote another draft. He didn't like it anymore. 'Sorry.' Miramax loved it, set up a meeting and then called Philippa's mobile to cancel it as we were walking into the building. Someone there was worried how I would get the double storyline on the screen. Amazing what minor details people will allow themselves to get worked up about! I started to get asked this a lot. 'How will people know which "story" is which?' I tried to explain in the most eloquent cinematic fashion I could muster given that I didn't really have the foggiest. 'Hmm. I see . . . well . . .' Apathy. My hot script was starting to cool down.

The only plus point at this stage was that the actor John Hannah had read it and said he desperately wanted to play the male lead and would do it for nothing if necessary. Good solidarity which was needed at the time. Poor John didn't realise that there was a chance his magnanimous attitude could end up biting him in the wallet as we were running out of places to go for cash.

You can't simply fly in the face of criticism – especially when it starts to acquire a consistency. I went back to the script again and again – with the help of Philippa and my best mate and business partner Douglas McFerran, who ended up playing Russell in the film. We were on draft five by now – constantly trying to make it clearer how it would work on the screen.

The main problem was that by now everyone had read it, loved it, questioned it and gone off it – so getting them to read it *again* was going to be tricky. In fact it proved mainly impossible. They're just 'too busy'. Fair enough, but we were quite simply running out of options and my sizzling hot script was now in the early stages of hypothermia – and it was looking terminal.

An actress friend of mine who had started to have some serious film success in the States had said that she would like to play the lead part and we could use her name to help the cause. This did help us to get interest eventually from a couple of private financiers who said they would pay for the film (then budgeted at about $1.5m) between them as long as we had this actress. Terms were tentatively agreed in principle although nothing was signed, so we called up and made an offer only to be told she had been advised to stay in Hollywood for now and not come to England to do a small UK picture. You've never seen a playground empty so fast. All the 'money' simply disappeared. No one seemed to have enough confidence in the script – or me and Philippa, either alone or as a package. No named star. No cash.

Personally I wasn't phased by this. I was in a mindset now that I have never experienced in my life. Suddenly I understood expressions like 'blind determination'. I kept telling Philippa that – as with the message the film has – everything, even bad news was happening ultimately for the best and if we could somehow trust in that we would not be able to fail. It can be a tough one to hang on to, but we stuck together. Philippa had now put a year and a half of her life into this and had been unstinting in her tenacity and faith – so I was partly determined not to give in for her. We had become a very close team.

We tried desperately to find someone else that our potential financiers would be happy with as a replacement. They wouldn't bite on anyone and no one seemed to be able to agree on anything suddenly. Eventually it all collapsed in on itself and Philippa and I were back at square one – it had taken fifteen months to get precisely nowhere.

So, on June 11 1996 my staying power took a serious dip and I went off to the pub to drown my sorrows with champagne and Guinness. I wasn't going to make my film after all. It simply wasn't meant to be.

Just as I started to quoff my third pint Philippa came running into the pub. 'Howitt, put that Guinness down – Sydney Pollack wants to talk to you!' Gulp! *The Sydney Pollack*, a film maker whose efforts such as *The Way We Were, Out of Africa, Tootsie, Three Days of the Condor* had only managed to procure him a measly *forty-six* Academy Award nominations, had read the script and called Philippa out of the blue.

Instantly sober we hurried back to Philippa's office in Oxford Street to call Sydders. It turns out that John Hannah had been visiting in LA meeting producers and serious people and in general conversation mentioned the film and its premise to Sydney and Lindsay Doran, then at Sydney's company Mirage Enterprises – and they liked the sound of it. John happened to have a copy of the script in his bag and gave it to them to read. Fate, finally was starting to play its part.

Sydney said he, Lindsay and Bill Horberg his other partner loved the script and asked if he could have a few days to try to raise the money. 'Go on then, Syd, as it's you.' And in a few days that's exactly what he did. He made one phone call to Guy East at Intermedia Films – Guy read it. We were summoned to his office for a grilling. 'How will we know which story we're watching?' – Oh, *that* old chestnut. I was so top at answering that one by now I had applied to Mastermind to answer questions on it.

Philippa and I flew to New York to meet Sydney, Lindsay and Bill for a script session. They had loads of great notes – and some that highlighted the US/UK cultural divide. 'What is Bradford?' was one of Lindsay's early enquiries. But they were so good at story and homing in on where the structure and development were not all they could be. They made minutely specific points on everything and anything that bothered them. I kept writing and re-writing. Drafts nine, ten, eleven came in quick succession.

In October 1996 Douglas McFerran and I bought economy tickets to Los Angeles – a place I had promised myself I would never visit and ironically two years later from where I am writing this article. We checked into the Hotel Carmel in Santa Monica – a cheap and cheerful *Barton Fink* type of place – and the next day I drove to Paramount Studios for more script meetings with the Mirage tribe. I tried to be really cool driving through the famous Melrose gate but I'm a Brit from Manchester so I failed miserably.

We were now starting to cast the film as well as continuing to hone in on the script, constantly questioning it and refusing to pretend something worked that didn't. 'Where are you going to do your writing?' Sydney asked me. I told him we had this little hotel that has a small round table in the room and I would work there. Sydney suddenly slapped his forehead as if swatting an imaginary fly. 'I'm going crazy – you know I keep forgetting – I have this beach house in Malibu – I never use it – why don't you work there?' Nothing odd about this. We all have beach houses somewhere that have slipped our minds. 'Sydney,' I said, 'why don't I *stay* there?' 'I was just going to say that.' 'I accept.' I drove back to Santa Monica and met Doug in the Second Street Bar and Grill. 'Pack up – we're moving to Malibu!'

We drove up the Pacific Highway the next day. Sydney was there making the place tidy. He showed us where everything was. It was beautiful. The Pacific Ocean lapped underneath the sun-drenched verandah. Sydney told me it was here that he, Dustin Hoffman and Larry Gelbert had spent three months carving out the story for *Tootsie*, one of my favourite films. That made me so excited. I was going to write my script in the same room! Sydney left – Doug and I walked around for a few seconds trying to be laid back – then we looked at each other and burst out laughing like a couple of kids. This was seriously heady stuff.

All the LA agents were sending the script out to their top clients. Lindsay took me round to meet them all. Rick Kurtzman at CAA said he wanted to show the script to Gwyneth Paltrow and thought she would like it. He did. She did. She signed up to play the lead. Immediately every major studio wanted to distribute the film. Paramount and Miramax eventually bought the film jointly, Miramax taking US domestic and Paramount all other English speaking territories.

It is very hard to describe how this all felt suddenly after the disappointments we had had to endure. It really was a game of two halves. The day before Sydney called we were 5–0 down at home to Welling United. Now it looked like we might win the European Cup.

Philippa and I had taken fifteen months to get zero finance in the UK. Sydney Pollack took fifteen days to get the film fully financed – in the UK! With the first draft being completed on January 15 1995, fifteen had become the common denominator. The fact that the film finally premiered at the Sundance Film festival on January 15 this year seems quite fitting. It was exactly three years to the day.

Peter Howitt
Extracts of this introduction first appeared in
The Sunday Telegraph

Sliding Doors

BLACK SCREEN

FADE UP CAPTION

> 'There are things known and
> things unknown . . . and in-between
> . . . The doors'
> Aldous Huxley

INT. BEDROOM. DAY

A hand knocks over a cup of tea on the corner of a dressing table spilling some tea onto the book *To Kill a Mockingbird* by Harper Lee.

A wrist is held up to reveal a watch telling us it is 9.47 a.m.

CLOSE SHOT: Helen. She is a woman in her mid to late 20s. This is her story. She curses the time, and the bedroom door shuts as she leaves.

In the background her boyfriend Gerry sleeps on in bed.

EXT. LONDON SKYLINE. DAY

A big landscape of London centring on the Houses of Parliament, the Embankment and the Thames. End on Embankment underground station.

INT. TUBE STATION PLATFORM. DAY

A tube train's sliding doors open and out of them comes a hurried Helen.

INT. BIG CLOSE SHOT:

A Woman of 29 (Lydia) applying lipstick.

INT. GERRY'S FLAT. BATHROOM. DAY

The sliding doors to a shower open and the upper body of a man in his late 20s gets in (Gerry).

3

EXT. EMBANKMENT TUBE STATION. DAY

Helen enters Villiers Street. She dials a number on a mobile phone as she hurries up the road.

INT. SANDWICH BAR. DAY

The 60-year-old Owner of the sandwich bar picks up the phone. He nods, says OK and puts down the phone. He starts to brew a coffee.

INT. BIG CLOSE SHOT:

A woman's long black coat is being buttoned up.

EXT. SANDWICH BAR. DAY

The Owner is standing in the doorway holding out a takeaway coffee and a snack in a white paper bag. Helen comes past and grabs them on the move, smiling and blowing him a kiss 'thank you' as she carries on. He smiles affectionately at her.

There is a 'Staff Wanted' sign in the window.

INT. GERRY'S FLAT. LIVING ROOM. DAY

CLOSE SHOT: A hand goes into a classic silk-lined box and two sumptuous Waterford crystal brandy glasses are taken out.

    CUT TO:

INT. GERRY'S FLAT. HALLWAY. DAY

Gerry, towel round his waist, carries the glasses and a bottle of brandy on a tray down the corridor of the flat to the bedroom.

EXT. LONDON SUBURBAN STREET. DAY

A pair of black high-heeled shoes are swung into a VW Golf and the car door is shut. The car moves off.

EXT. CHARING CROSS ROAD. DAY

Helen comes hastily out of an off-licence with two carrier bags and hurries up Charing Cross Road.

EXT. LONDON STREETS. DAY

The VW Golf continues along the road.

EXT. OFFICE BLOCK. DAY

Helen enters the office.

INT. LONDON OFFICE RECEPTION AREA. DAY

CLOSE SHOT: the light at the top of the lift as it comes on and the lift sliding doors open. Helen comes out and goes into the main office.

END OF TITLE SEQUENCE

INT. LONDON PR OFFICE. DAY

As Helen enters the office the five or so desks in the open plan area are empty. The 'team' are gathered in the glass-walled conference room at the end of the office.

Helen ups her pace through the office, dumping her coffee and snack on her desk as she goes. She still has the carrier bags.

> HELEN
> (*to herself*)
> Shit shit shit shit shit, tchoh shit.
> (*she mimics*)
> 'Hello, Helen, I'd almost forgotten you work here.'

She goes into the conference room.

Five Men sit round the table in shirt-sleeves. They are stony-faced. There is an almost self-assured smug look about a few of them.

The Boss (Paul) speaks.

PAUL

Hi, Helen . . .

HELEN

. . . I know, I know, you'd almost forgotten I worked here, but I swear I was up all night toying with the fashion show and I've really hit on something . . . you see . . .

She takes in their faces for the first time.

What?

Paul picks up an empty spirits crate. Helen gets the reference at once.

I took four bottles of vodka on Friday. It was my birthday. You know that. I was having a party. I was running late so I borrowed some . . .

PAUL

Not a lot of use to me when I had nothing to offer the executives who called by unexpectedly late Friday evening.

HELEN

Off the top of my head you could have told them you'd run out. It's popular stuff, been sending a lot round to people, real buzz about it, etc., etc., bullshit bullshit. We're in PR. That's what we do, isn't it?

She looks at his face. He is resolute – unmoved. The reality of the situation hits her immediately.

But you didn't do that, did you, Paul? No no. So I'm out, am I? Well this is perfect, isn't it? Congratulations. You've wanted me out for ages. Now you did it. Very well done. Theft. Yeah pretty foolproof. OK. I'll go, I'll go. I was getting a bit choked up with all the testosterone flying about the place. Best I get out before I start growing a penis.

She leaves. A moment of silence.

                    STEVE
  Told you – lesbian.

  CUT TO:

INT. LONDON OFFICE RECEPTION AREA. DAY

Helen walks out through the main reception area. She presses the
lift button.

Despite her clinical tirade she suddenly looks deflated and defeated.
Lost.

The lift has arrived. The sliding doors open. Already in the lift are
a group of three or four Businessmen who have come from an
office above.

One of them is James Hammerton a handsome 32-year-old. He is
in seemingly high spirits. Another young Businessman is with him.

                    JAMES
  I thought they would be much harder to crack than that. Hah!

Helen gets into the lift. She runs her hand through her hair. As she
does she dislodges one of her earrings. It falls to the floor by
James's feet. He instinctively picks it up and hands it to her.

She doesn't register him.

                    HELEN
  Thanks.

The sliding doors of the lift are shut.

INT. GERRY'S FLAT. BATHROOM. DAY

Gerry stands with a towel round his waist looking in the mirror.
The front door bell buzzes.

Gerry moves quickly through the bedroom. He moves the alarm

7

clock on the side of the bed round so he can see the dial.
11.32 a.m.

CUT TO:

INT. GERRY'S FLAT. FRONT DOOR. DAY

The front door as Gerry opens it.

A pair of black high-heeled shoes walk in past Gerry's bare feet. They stop and turn. We travel up the body of the Woman (Lydia) as she starts to unbutton her long black coat.

Gerry closes the door.

Lydia lets her coat fall to the ground. We see all of her for the first time. She is wearing *only* black high-heeled shoes and a pair of black French knickers.

She leans forward and pulls free the towel from around his waist and lets it fall to the ground.

On Gerry.

EXT. OFFICE. LONDON. DAY

Helen walks out of the building and walks off down Charing Cross Road. She is in a world of her own. Just in front of her James is walking in the same direction.

INT. EMBANKMENT UNDERGROUND. DAY

Helen heads through the barrier. She gets onto the escalator down towards the District Line.

We can see James at the bottom of the escalator as he disappears round onto the platform.

A third of the way down Helen hears the tube train thundering into the station. She starts to run down the escalator to try to catch the train.

She gets to the bottom and runs round through the small tunnel onto the platform just as the sliding doors of the tube train are starting to close.

A Mother and 2-year-old Child are in the tunnel, having just got off the train, as Helen runs through.

The 2-year-old Child wanders over into Helen's path and she has to check herself briefly so as not to send the child flying. She hardly breaks her stride.

However this split second makes all the difference and she is just too late arriving on the platform and the sliding doors shut just as she gets to them.

Important visual sequence

Immediate cut back to:

Int. Embankment Underground. Day

Helen coming down the escalator as before (same footage). The sound of the train again and Helen runs down the escalator and round onto the platform again as the sliding doors of the tube train are shutting.

The Mother and 2-year-old Child are there as before.

This time the Mother pulls the Child towards her out of Helen's path and she gets a clean run at the train. She arrives at the train just as the sliding doors are closing and makes a desperate lunge for the train. She just manages to stop the door with her arm and a Man on the train helps prise it open for her. She gets on.

(N.B. This is an integral moment. From now on we will follow the two stories of Helen. The one that missed the train and the one that caught it.

For ease of differentiation the story of Helen who missed the train will be written in normal print – and the story of Helen who caught the train in a different type face.

9

INT. EMBANKMENT TUBE PLATFORM. DAY

Helen watches as the train starts to pull out.

Int. tube train. Day

Helen takes off her coat and settles down in a seat of the fairly crowded train. Next to her James has just sat down. There is no recognition between them.

INT. EMBANKMENT TUBE PLATFORM. DAY

Helen watching the train moving off.

Int. Embankment tube platform. Day

Helen and James are seated together as the train moves off.

Int. tube train. Day

The train windows go black as the train hits the tunnel.

INT. EMBANKMENT TUBE PLATFORM. DAY

Helen waits on the platform. She looks up at the information board. No trains are showing. The Tannoy voice comes on.

> TANNOY
> (*voice-over*)
> District Line information. Due to an earlier incident at Mile end, District Line westbound trains are subject to a delay. We apologise for . . .

Helen doesn't wait to hear the last bit. She leaves the station.

EXT. STREET. DAY

Helen stands on the side of the street hailing a taxi. A taxi indicates he is pulling in for her.

Suddenly from nowhere a hand tries to grab her bag and open it at the same time. The contents spill out on the pavement.

In her attempt to thwart the attacker Helen falls and hits her head on the corner of the pavement. The taxi has pulled up and the Cabbie jumps out as the attacker runs off into the crowd.

The Cabbie runs to comfort Helen. She is checking her bag. Her head is bleeding.

> CABBIE
>
> You all right, love?

> HELEN
>
> Bastards got my video membership card. Ah, serves them right. Let them pay the fine.

> CABBIE
>
> That's a nasty cut. You'll need a couple of stitches. Come on, get in.

He helps Helen into the cab.

Int. Gerry's flat. Bedroom. Day

Gerry and Lydia stand close together. They are naked. They both hold a glass which Gerry fills with brandy. They stare steamily at each other. The talk is casual but charged. They kiss each other lightly as they speak.

> **Lydia**
>
> I never figured out why we didn't make it, Gerry.

> **Gerry**
>
> You went home to America, remember? I couldn't afford the bus fares.

> **Lydia**
>
> But I came back, huh? I turn my back for three lousy years and you callously ditch me for another woman.

> **Gerry**
>
> I know, I'm just naturally impetuous, I suppose.

Lydia

I like it like this though. No pressure – no 'shopping' – just . . .
brandy.

Lydia takes a sensual sip from her glass and then kisses Gerry,
allowing the brandy to run out of her mouth and down her upper
body, which we don't see. Gerry's head leaves frame as he begins to
lick the spilt brandy from Lydia's breast. Close in on her face as her
head goes back with electric sexual pleasure.

Gerry's hand appears on her shoulder and pulls her out of shot.

The sound of a Man singing.

Man

(*voice-over*)

'He's dragged me to the floor.'

Int. tube train. Day

On the train the Man sings along annoyingly to his Walkman. Helen
reads her book. It has a nasty tea stain in the corner which has
soaked several pages.

James looks at the Man.

James

Oohoo. Beatle lyrics.

The Man takes off his Walkman headphones.

Man

What?

James looks at the cassette box.

James

Elastic Thrombosis, they're guilty of lyric poaching.

James looks at Helen.

James
(to Helen)
They're Beetle's lyrics aren't they?

Helen
I don't know, sorry.

James
Course you do. Everyone is born knowing all the Beatles lyrics instinctively. They're passed into the foetus subconsciously with all the amniotic stuff. Fact they should be called The Foetles.

Nothing from Helen. The Man puts his headphones back on.

Hmm, not a fan, clearly.

INT. HOSPITAL CASUALTY. DAY

Helen is being 'handed over' by the kind Cabbie to a Casualty Doctor. She thanks him. He winks and wishes her well and leaves.

Int. tube train. Day

A few stops later. The train is pulling out of a station. Helen sits looking at but not reading her book.

James
Funny the way nobody speaks on tubes, isn't it? I mean I rarely catch the tube but . . . Or in lifts. Confined spaces, everybody shuts down. Why is that? Perhaps we think everyone else on the tube or in the lift is a potential psychopath. Or a drunk. So we close down and pretend to read a book or something. You've got a tea stain on your book, by the way.

Helen
(dismissively)
Look I don't think you're a psychopath. I just want to read my book.

James

I understand. I apologise. I'm er . . . I'm in a little bit of a good mood as a matter of fact, today, so, er . . . sorry.

Helen

It's OK.

Although overly chatty there is something inoffensive and unobtrusive about James. He looks around at other Passengers.

A moment passes. He glances at Helen again.

James

Did you know the bloke who lives in the flat above me used to be married to Harper Lee's cousin's next door neighbour's hairdresser? Something like that.

She looks at him.

Sorry. Sorry. – Have we met before? No, I . . . honestly, you seem familiar.

Helen

I don't think so.

He notices her earring.

James

Yes, yes, you were in the lift, just now, you dropped your earring. I picked it up.

Helen

Oh yes, you did. Thank you.

James

Pleasure. You work there?

She looks at him hard for a moment.

Helen

I did do. But I have just been fired. OK?

James

Oh no, that's . . . that's horrible. I'm sorry.

Helen

That's OK. You didn't do it. Now thank you for your concern, I'm glad you're in a good mood, etc., and thank you for picking up my earring but I just want to read my book.

INT. HOSPITAL CASUALTY. DAY

In a small cubicle Helen is finishing having a bandage fitted to her slight head wound by the Casualty Doctor.

Int. tube. Day

The tube train pulls into Fulham Broadway Station

James

Well, I get off here – I'm just telling you in case you get off here too and you get up before me and then I get up and you think I'm following you. Which I'm not, I mean I wouldn't, I mean, you know . . .

     (suddenly he is very serious and genuine)

I really didn't mean any offence. Please forgive me. I'm really not a nutcase. I apologise.

He gets up. Heads for the doors. Helen gets up too and gets off as he does, slightly behind him.

Int. Fulham Broadway Station. Day

Helen

Excuse me.

He turns round.

    I . . . er . . . look I'm sorry, I'm sure you're not a nutcase or a psycho or anything . . . I just . . . I'm not that . . . er . . . good at . . . er you know er . . .

James

Constructing sentences?

She laughs.

Helen

Talking. On tubes. You're right. No one does it. And I'm a little
. . . you know. Er . . . so . . . anyway . . .

She goes slightly distant.

James

You live in Fulham?

Helen

Hmmm?

James

Is this your stop? Only you got off the train. This is Fulham
Broadway.

Helen

Yes. Yes I live just up the road.

James

Me too. I'm James.

Helen

Helen.

James

Hi, Helen. Walk you to the street?

She giggles foolishly and they walk off. After a few silent steps,
suddenly Helen blurts out.

Helen

I live with someone. A man. I live with a man.

James

Really. I have people I consider soul mates who don't confide in
me this much. And what would he think if he knew you were

walking up from the tube in broad daylight with a complete stranger? Pretty outrageous stuff.

Helen laughs. A moment.

Helen
OK. You are clearly not in the mood to be deterred so . . . I'm curious, how come you're in such a good mood?

James
Well . . . barring a disaster I may well have just become the sole British franchise licence-holder of a large and successful American sports company. So after a period in my life in which everything seemed to be going wrong suddenly everything seems to be going OK. See, now I'm confiding in you. So don't worry about losing your job, they're plainly not aware of your amazing potential and I know some of my good fortune will rub off on you and now we're at the exit and I go left. It was nice to meet you, Helen. I'm sorry about your job. Really. I suppose being Aquarian can have its down-sides.

They have indeed reached the exit. As he wanders off he turns back.

You know what the Monty Python boys say?

Helen
What? 'Always look on the bright side of life'?

James
No – no one expects the Spanish Inquisition.

He waves and walks off. Helen looks after him.

Helen
(*to herself*)
He's a bloody nutter.
(*calling*)
Hey, how did you know I was an Aquarian?

Without turning back James holds his arms out in a 'don't ask me' fashion.

Int. bedroom. Gerry's flat. Day

The sexual festivities continue with vigour and fervency. Gerry's leg swings round and unbeknownst to him knocks the phone by the side of the bed off the hook. Lydia pins him down on the bed and puts her face close.

Lydia
I never stopped loving you, Gerry.

She plants her mouth firmly on his in a passionate kiss. The sex continues.

EXT. STREET. (NEAR CASUALTY.) DAY

Helen is dialling on her mobile phone. She gets the engaged signal.

VISUAL NOTE: she now has a small bandage on her forehead. This will differentiate her from Helen visually.

Helen puts down her receiver.

Int. Gerry's flat. Day

The key in the door as Helen enters. She is about to call out when she notices the towel on the floor by the door and then her gaze wanders to the discarded coat.

She can hear the sound of Elton John's 'Funeral for a Friend' coming from the bedroom.

She walks slowly along past the living room, kitchen and to the bedroom door which is just open. She can hear the soft moans of a man and woman inside.

She pushes the door open and walks in and stands by the door.

On the bed Gerry is sitting with Lydia astride him; they are rocking back and forth like a rocking chair. Gerry facing Helen, Lydia has her back to her. Gerry's eyes are closed as he is reaching towards climax. He is moaning. As he rocks back and forth his voice gets louder and louder.

Gerry

Oh yeah . . . Hmmm . . . Oh . . . Ohho . . . Oh yes indeed . . . Oh yes . . . Oh Yes! *Oh yes!! . . . Oh Yesss!!! . . . Ohhh Yessss!!!!!*

He opens his eyes and sees Helen looking at him.

. . . Oh fuck!!!

His movement immediately stops as he is frozen in the headlights of Helen's eyes. Lydia keeps going.

Lydia

Yes, yes – talk to me like that. Tell me again. Don't stop . . . Oh please don't stop . . . Please . . . Oh.

Gerry is tapping her on the shoulder to get her attention. Her cries eventually subside and she looks at him, sees him staring and looks round to see Helen.

Lydia just looks at Helen, stony-faced. A long moment of silence. Eventually.

Helen
(*casually*)

I didn't think you liked Elton John.

Gerry
(*trance-like*)

I do sometimes.

Helen

Yeah? Just shows, you never really know people, do you? Go ahead, tell her again. She's right, you really shouldn't just stop like that. Set a woman back three days doing a thing like that. Who is she?

Lydia
(unfazed)

She's Lydia.

Helen moves her stare to Lydia. A moment of eyeballing. Lydia then calmly picks up her knickers and leaves, unruffled.

A beat. The sound of the front door closing. Another beat.

Helen

Well, I've had a dreadful day. I got sacked. And so did you, it would seem. Cup of tea?

She turns and casually walks out of the door leaving Gerry still staring pathetically.

Suddenly she comes back through the door at speed and launches herself on the bed at him like a missile screaming and punching him.

You bastard. You useless shagging man-type bastard. You bastard. You bastard . . . you bastard . . . you bastard . . .

She gets slower and slower until there is almost a macabre Hannibal Lecter-style calm rhythm to her beating which accompanies the word 'bastard' each time.

INT. TAXI CAB. DAY

Helen sits in the taxi on her way home. Her head bandaged.

Int. Gerry's flat. Day

Helen
(vehemently)

Try not to over-react?!! Try not . . . !! You haven't laid a finger on me in two months – two months, Gerry. Almost to the day. I am working all the hours under the sun to support you while you are supposedly writing your first novel, I come home and catch you up to your nuts in Lady Shagging Godiva and yet I should 'try – not – to – over-react'?!! Like I don't have a point? Is that

22

what you're saying? Is it? I have a point, Gerry! Believe me – I have a very big point. I have such a big point I could shove it right through you and make a kebab out of you. Am I being clear-ish?

Gerry

Look . . . look . . .

He goes into a thought process. Helen watches. Eventually.

Helen

Yes? Look . . . ? That's not much of a sentence, is it? 'Look look', is it? It's just two words. It's just one word, in fact, repeated. Look – what?

Gerry

No, it's all right - nothing.

Helen

'Look . . . look . . . no it's all right nothing'?!! Oh dear, your knob's gone soft but now your brain's got a stiffy. How long? Huh? Do you love her? No, don't tell me. I'm not interested – No, do tell me. I am interested. Hmm? Questions too difficult? I'm only asking because I need to know exactly how big a mug I am. Hmmm?

But he simply can't speak. She picks up her coat and heads for the door. She looks at him for a moment. He seems unable to function at all.

She leaves the room. The sound of the door slamming. Gerry sits down on the bed and sees an earring that Lydia left behind. He picks it up and holds it.

EXT. GERRY'S FLAT. DAY

The door to the flat closes and Lydia comes out. Panning to the window we see Gerry waving her goodbye. They are both exuding sexually fulfilled radiance.

23

Lydia gets into her VW Golf and drives off.

She drives down the road to the junction of the main road. As she turns the corner the cab with Helen in pulls into the road. The two cars pass each other.

The cab continues along to the flat and Helen gets out and goes to the front door.

The next-door neighbour is kneeling, scrubbing her doorstep as if possessed. As she scrubs she is yelling and screaming at someone in the house in German.

Helen lets herself in.

INT. GERRY'S FLAT. DAY

Helen comes into the flat. The sound of water splashing down from a shower.

CUT TO:

In the bathroom Gerry is showering himself off. He hears the door shut and pulls back the sliding doors to see who it is. Cut between the bathroom and Helen moving through the flat to join him.

>HELEN

Hello . . . Gerry?

>GERRY
>(*calling*)

Helen, that you?

>HELEN
>(*playfully*)
No, it's your bit of stuff. Wednesday – shag day, remember?

>GERRY
>(*to himself*)

Jesus Christ.

He slams the shower sliding doors shut and instinctively grabs the soap and frantically starts scrubbing his balls like a madman.

Helen has made it to the bedroom and calls through to the bathroom, taking in the dishevelled state of the bed.

> HELEN
> Have you just got up, you lazy git?

Gerry gets out of the shower, thinking madly on his feet.

> GERRY
> Yeah . . . yeah . . . I er . . . I didn't sleep that well, you know er . . . then I went into a deep . . . really, er, deep, deep sleep when you left for some er . . . you know . . . I think I might be coming down with er . . . anyway what are you doing home at . . .

Gerry arrives in the bedroom with a towel round him and sees the bandage on her head.

> . . . Oh my God, what happened to you?

> HELEN
> Huh, well, depends. Which story do you want first?

The radio is on and Elton John has just come on singing 'Honkey Cat'.

> GERRY
> Eh?

> HELEN
> Well, I . . .

Gerry suddenly sees one of Lydia's earrings on the bed. He launches himself onto the bed like a rocket and grabs it.

> What are you doing?

Gerry instinctively turns off the radio.

Can't stand Elton John, you know that. Anyway, look – what happened? What's happened to your head?

He gets up and crosses to her, dropping the earring in the bin at the side of the bed as he does.

HELEN
Well, I got mugged and sacked . . . Only not in that order.

Gerry is now into the concerned boyfriend role, convinced he has had the escape of the century.

GERRY
What! . . . You . . .

HELEN
Well, I mean I was sacked first and mugged later, although it wasn't an actual mugging it was only an 'attempted' mugging, according to the policeman because they, er . . . they didn't . . .

She is beginning to crumble with the shock of it all.

GERRY
Wait wait – whoah, whoah, slow down – stop, wait a sec, wait a sec. OK. Come here. Just . . .

He puts his arm round her and takes her to the bed and sits her down. He is kissing her gently on the cheek.

That's it. Now then, just relax – take a deep breath. OK, just . . . Take it easy, you've obviously had a bit of a shock,
(she's not the only one)
. . . You're in shock, sweetheart. Now then . . . there we are. OK? Now then.

He looks up and sees the brandy bottle on the dressing table with the *two glasses* by the side of it. He leaps up instinctively.

Do you want a brandy?

He crosses to the dressing table where the brandy and two glasses are. He grabs one of them and chucks it neatly into the washing basket next to the dressing table.

> HELEN
>
> It's four in the afternoon.

> GERRY
>
> Course it is. Sorry.

Gerry has unknowingly poured himself a massive one and takes a large calming swig from it without knowing he is doing it. Helen looks at him.

> HELEN
>
> Gerry! Are you OK?

> GERRY
>
> Me? Fine. Fine. I'm just er . . . hmhmmm bit of a chest cold . . . Now – tell me all about it.

Ext. Albert Bridge. Day

Helen, tears rolling down her cheeks, is looking out over the Thames. A rowing 8 passes her under the bridge. A courting Couple walk past, arm in arm. A Jogger runs past and a 6-year-old Boy runs by with a kite followed by his Mum trying to keep up. Life goes on. Helen takes off a ring that Gerry bought her and throws it in the river.

INT. GERRY'S FLAT. DAY

Gerry has managed to get back in control of the situation. Helen finishes telling him her story.

> HELEN
>
> . . . and then I waited hours in Casualty and I had to give a statement and all that and I couldn't help thinking if I'd have just caught that bloody train it would never have happened. I'd have been home ages ago and . . .

Gerry has immediately imagined what that would have meant (we, of course, have seen it). He jumps in.

GERRY

Well look you mustn't think like that. You can't go round wondering 'what if this', you know, 'if only that'. It's done now. Come on. I'm going to – Follow.

He leads her into the bathroom and runs the water in the sink.

Splash . . .

She splashes her face.

. . . Going to take you out and get you alarmingly out of your head on Grolsch and . . . Dry . . .

He hands her the towel and she dries her face.

. . . and then – this way –
(*leading her to her wardrobe and opening it*)
– and then when you've sung all your favourite Barbra Streisand songs at the top of your voice and got us slung out of the pub – put this on . . .
(*taking a dress out of the wardrobe and handing it to her*)
. . . I'm going to let you have carnal knowledge of a lamb passanda – which I know your diet does not allow – with double tarka dahl, which you can then throw up all over the pristine doorstep of Herr and Frau Goebbels next door. Chop chop.

Helen is laughing at him. She throws her arms around him.

HELEN

Oh I love you, Gerry.

Gerry's face over her shoulder!

SMASH CUT TO:

Ext. Anna's flat. Evening

Close shot: of Anna, who is Helen's best friend. A woman of about thirty.

Anna
Gerry, she's not here!

She is standing on her doorstep talking to Gerry. She is unsympathetic to his frantic state.

Gerry
Oh, come on, Anna, you're Helen's best friend, where else would she be?

Anna
Come in and search the place if you like. She's not here, Gerry. What is it you've done anyway? Can't have been very nice if she's walked out on you.

He has no desire to answer.

Gerry
OK. Sorry, well if she comes here will you just let me know or get her to ring or something? That's all I ask.

Anna
Like you say, Gerry, I'm Helen's best friend. If she comes here I'll do what she asks.

She shuts the door in his face.

Int. Bertorelli's Wine Bar and Bistro. Night

Helen sits with a bottle of Grolsch beer. She lights a cigarette.

Int. local pub. Night

Gerry sits with his mate Russell. They are in mid discussion.

Russell
Well, she's got a point.

(Gerry looks at him)

You can't stand Elton John.

Gerry

Russell, forget Elton John. What do I do?

Russell

Gerry, you've been telling me for weeks that you couldn't hack it juggling between Helen and Lydia. That you wished you hadn't got involved with her again.

Gerry

I know.

Russell

And that you didn't think you were cut out for infidelity.

Gerry

I know.

Russell

But you couldn't end it with Lydia because you weren't sure how she'd take it.

Gerry

Yes. I know all this.

Russell

And I told you that something – if you remember my words – 'ungoverned by you' would happen to bring the situation to a head.

Gerry

I know.

Russell

And something has. Ha ha.

He bursts into hysterics.

Gerry

It's not funny actually, Russell.

Russell

No, sorry I beg to differ, old man, it's very, very, very funny. And look at you. It's not as if you're running around frantically looking for her.

Gerry

I went to Anna's. She wasn't there.

Russell

You went to Anna's! Boy you're a regular one-man SAS crack unit. Want my opinion?

Gerry

Will I like it?

Russell

Course not – it'll be based on reality.

Gerry sinks his head in his hands on the table.

(Important visual sequence: following three scenes.)

Int. Bertorelli's. Evening

Helen sits with another bottle of Grolsch and lights another cigarette.

Unseen by Helen, through the window James is coming along the road with a male Friend (Clive). They come into the wine bar and up to the bar, not seeing Helen at first.

Clive

No, no, you don't advertise a new restaurant. Very uncool. It's word of mouth. People talk.

James

And how do these people who talk know where you are so they can talk about you? Hey, listen, it's your restaurant, Clive, I just . . .

He sees Helen at the bar, staring down at her cigarette as if it holds the answer to her problem. She has obviously been crying.

Helen. Hello. James. Rather annoying chatty bloke on the tube?

Helen looks up. She takes a moment to realise who he is.

Helen
(*almost inaudible*)
Oh . . . yes . . . Hi.

She takes an amateur drag of her cigarette. Her hand is trembling slightly.

He goes over to her.

James
Oh dear. You look all stressed up with nowhere to go. It's only a job, you'll get another one.

Helen looks up at him.

It's something else, isn't it? Sometimes helps to just say whatever it is out loud.

Helen doesn't speak.

Of course it also helps if people mind their own business and leave you alone. I'm sorry.

Helen
When I left you at the tube earlier I went home and found my boyfriend . . .

James/Helen
. . . in bed with another woman.

James
Shit! I mean, sorry. Er, oh dear. That is . . . what an idiot!

Helen
It's OK. You weren't to know.

James
Not me. Your boyfriend. He's an idiot. Er . . . I'm sorry. It's not my place. I . . .

Helen
It's OK. Thank you.

James
Well, look, if it makes you feel any better – see that bloke over there?
(points at Clive)
Not only does he own a personalised matching set of crocodile-skin luggage but his favourite programme is *Baywatch* – so, you see, there is always someone sadder than you.

She can't help laughing.

Do you love him?

Helen
No, I could never love a *Baywatch* fan.

James
Hey, you did a joke in the midst of your turbulent emotional state, that's very positive. Your boyfriend.

Helen
Ex-boyfriend. I don't know. No. Yes. We had been having er . . . well you know . . . We, er, oh . . . I don't know. Why am I telling you all this anyway?

James
Telling me all what? All I got then was that 'you and he were . . . er you . . . um, you know . . . er . . . um!' Listen, I'm celebrating, you're hurting, let's team up, we can . . . 'hurtibrate'.

She laughs again. Then looks at him.

Helen
Are you faithful to your girlfriend?

James checks himself slightly.

James
Well – er . . . actually at this precise moment I don't have a

girlfriend. But . . . er, infidelity happens to be something I don't particularly approve of. But don't be fooled. That doesn't mean I'm honourable necessarily. No no. When nobody's looking I pick my nose and flick it at the homeless and I'm on first name terms with several people from Ipswich. So, anyway . . . blah blah blah – 'life goes on'. Which it does, by the way, although you may not think it just now. But that's the annoying thing about clichés, they're all true. Listen, decide you want company and we're just over here, OK? I'm really sorry, Helen.

She nods, embarrassed. He wanders off.

INT. BERTORELLI'S. NIGHT

Helen and Gerry come in and walk up to the bar next to James and Clive.

(IMPORTANT VISUAL NOTE: There is no recognition between them as James has not met Helen in this storyline.)

We see Helen, Gerry and further along the bar James and co. At the end of the bar there is of course no Helen.

> GERRY
> Two of your most disgustingly large Grolsches and a large Jack Daniels with ice, please, and she'll have the same.

We pan away from them and back to the door as:

Int. Bertorelli's. Night

Anna (Helen's friend) comes in and looks around the bar. She spots Helen in the corner on her own and goes over to her.

(Important visual note: As Anna arrives with Helen at the other end of the bar we see James and Co. but no Helen and Gerry.)

> **Anna**
> Gerry came looking for you. Is it what I think?

Helen

Depends. Is what you think that I walked in on him shagging Lydia in my bed and I walked out?

Anna

Pretty much.

Helen

Then yes.

It is all suddenly too much for Helen and she crumbles into a mess of tears and Anna holds her tight.

INT. BERTORELLI'S. NIGHT

Uproarious laughter. Wide on the bar with Helen and Gerry sitting down at a table. Gerry is animated and Helen is laughing hysterically at him. In the background at the other side of the bar there is no Helen and Anna.

At the bar James and Clive stand drinking champagne. Gerry's mobile phone rings. He answers.

LYDIA
(*voice-over*)
This morning was sensational.

He neatly disconnects with his thumb and bluffs.

GERRY
Hello? Hello. Can't hear. Didn't know it was on.

He switches it off and puts it away. He picks up his Jack Daniels.

Ready steady go!

He downs it animatedly. Helen does the same. They laugh.

Landlord! Our firkins are dry. Send the wench with more ale. And two bags of ready salted.

They are in high spirits.

36

Int. Bertorelli's. Night

Later. No dialogue. Helen is now pretty drunk. James and Clive are just leaving. He looks over and waves goodbye to Helen. There is a moment. Helen smiles and waves back. Anna looks at him and immediately wants to know who this attractive man is. Helen drunkenly explains. They both watch him walk out of the bar.

Ext. Bertorelli's. Night

As Anna helps the wobbly Helen out of the bar James is just getting in a taxi. He leans out of the window.

James
Can I drop you off anywhere? Here, let me help you.

He gets out and helps Anna get Helen into the cab. Helen is very bendy.

Hey, hands up if you drank too much?

Helen
(*momentary drunken pomposity*)
I'm not as drunk as thinkle peep I am.

Anna
Put a wick in her mouth she'd burn for a fortnight.
(*to the Cabbie*)
Nine Menlove Avenue.
(*to James*)
Thanks a lot.

James
No bother.

The cab drives off.

Gerry and Helen have the remnants of a gargantuan Indian feast on their table.

> HELEN
> No more, really. I'll be sick.

> GERRY
> Well, we're on schedule for that but we've got to move locations so just don't swallow for ten minutes.

Int. Anna's flat. Spare bedroom. Night

Anna tucks a very drunk Helen into bed. She is chuntering drunkenly, half comatose.

> **Helen**
> He didn't fancy me. He was just being concerned.

> **Anna**
> Uhuh? Well, let me tell you if he was being that 'concerned' about me I wouldn't be helping you into bed right now.

> **Helen**
> Am I in bed?

> **Anna**
> Yes. Now sleep. You'll be fine.

> GERRY
> (*voice-over*)
> . . . just fine.

INT. GERRY'S BEDROOM. NIGHT

Helen's face as she is slopped over the shoulder of Gerry as he manoeuvres her into the bedroom and deposits her almost comatose body onto the bed.

> There we go.

Gerry for the first time shows the shock of his lucky escape. He walks into the bathroom.

He looks back at Helen fast asleep on the bed and shuts the door. He splashes his face with cold water and stares very closely at himself in the mirror.

> (*quietly intent*)
> OK. We are very overdue for a meeting. Question: Are you some peculiar, thus far undefined breed of dickhead? Hm? Are you? You Gerald Ashby have got two major, major head problems. One – that was close. It was too close. Put in layman's terms, she nearly caught you. You are getting sloppy. And two – and this is far more worrying than the first one – you are talking to yourself in the mirror again. Really bad sign.

He opens the bedroom door to look at Helen asleep on the bed.

MIX TO:

Int. Anna's flat. Spare bedroom. Night

Helen fast asleep in the bed.

Fade to black

(VISUAL NOTE: Throughout the following montage sequence Helen still has bandages and Band-aids on her forehead of increasingly small sizes as her wound heals.)

EXT. FULHAM. SKYLINE. DAY. MONTAGE

Fade up on the streets of London SW6.

EXT. GERRY'S FLAT. MORNING. MONTAGE

Outside Gerry's flat. The Postman leaves, having put letters through the letter box.

On the doorstep of the house next door is the German Woman (Frau Goebbels) who is throwing a bowl of hot water over her doorstep, to clean something off (Helen's sick). She is cursing vociferously in German.

INT. GERRY'S FLAT. BEDROOM. DAY. MONTAGE

Helen wakes up to Gerry holding out a glass of sparkling Redoxon orange Vitamin C drink. She holds out her hand for it without opening her eyes.

    MIX TO:

INT. GERRY'S FLAT. BATHROOM. DAY. MONTAGE

Helen showers herself. Eyes shut. Hungover. She has the bandage on her head still. Gerry opens the shower door to check on her. She is oblivious of him. He smiles. Shuts the shower door.

Int. Anna's flat. Bedroom. Day. Montage

Anna holds out a glass of strawberry drinking yoghurt. Helen reaches for it blindly and takes a sip. She pulls a face.

    Mix to:

Int. Anna's flat. Bathroom. Day

Helen showers. Establish that this is definitely not Gerry's flat. She turns off the shower and slides the door. Anna arrives with a warm towel.

INT. GERRY'S FLAT. BEDROOM/LIVING ROOM. DAY. MONTAGE

Helen walks through the bedroom in a robe. She glances momentarily at the dressing table wondering why something bothers her about it.

She walks through to the living room where Gerry sits at a typewriter typing away. He is surrounded by pieces of paper and

40

is deep at his work. He picks up a reference book.

Helen walks past him and waves pathetically at him – 'Yes, I'm walking, but that doesn't necessarily mean I'm alive.'

Gerry jumps up and grabs the wastepaper basket and walks in front of her holding it under her mouth. She slaps him playfully to stop it.

Ext. temp agency. Day. Montage

Helen looks at the lack of jobs on offer in the window.

INT. GERRY'S FLAT. LIVING ROOM/KITCHEN. DAY. MONTAGE

CLOSE SHOT: a page in the appointment section of the *Evening Standard* with various PR vacancies circled. They all have lines through them except for one. Helen (now with only a large plaster on her head) is on the phone nodding, resigned. She hangs up the phone and draws a line through the last vacancy.

INT. BERTORELLI'S. NIGHT. MONTAGE

Helen is handed a blue shirt with the bar logo on by the Boss. Helen smiles a dim smile of gratitude.

MIX TO:

INT. BERTORELLI'S. NIGHT. MONTAGE

Helen is wearing the polo shirt. It is her first session working at the bar. The place is fairly full. There is a band on stage (Those Magnificent Men).

She is busy, taking orders, delivering food and drinks, etc., in the restaurant and kitchen area.

She looks over at the Boss who nods at her. She is working well.

Int. Anna's flat. Day. Montage

Anna and Helen are sitting on the sofa looking at a hairstyle magazine. Helen shakes her head at the outrageous style on the open page.

Various shots of the pages turning, fingers pointing, Helen laughing, shaking her head, Anna pulling and manoeuvring Helen's hair into various shapes to copy the styles.

The phone rings. They stop dead and look at each other. Anna answers. Helen is tense. Anna shakes her head, it's not Gerry. Helen looks deflated.

INT. GERRY'S FLAT. LIVING ROOM. DAY. MONTAGE

In the kitchen Helen is loading up the washing machine. She is wearing a Walkman.

Gerry comes round the doorway with a briefcase in his hand and mouths 'I'm going to the library' and does a book opening mime. He blows a kiss. She waves 'bye' back at him.

As she empties the laundry basket she finds the brandy glass that Gerry discarded into it. Helen looks at it, slightly puzzled, then puts it on the draining-board.

INT. LYDIA'S FLAT. DAY. MONTAGE

ANGLE: on the floor a briefcase. The name in gold embossed letters on the side: GERRY ASHBY.

Panning off it and around the room to discarded clothes. Lydia's head and naked shoulders arrive at the end of the sofa. Her hair and face are sweaty. Her head disappears again.

INT. BERTORELLI'S. NIGHT. MONTAGE

The end of a session. Helen is slumped on a bar stool seeing off a large cold Coke.

The Boss gives her some money. She looks at the money in her hand. Her face shows that this job just isn't going to bring in enough cash on its own.

INT./EXT. SANDWICH SHOP. DAY. MONTAGE

The sandwich shop Owner takes the 'Staff Wanted' sign out of the window.

MIX TO:

Helen behind the counter making various sandwiches and loading them into a big basket. She refers to an order list. Her hair is tied back and she is being as industrious as she can.

EXT. STREET. DAY

Helen walks along with a sandwich basket on her arm.

INT. LONDON OFFICE. DAY. MONTAGE

Helen, a basket over her arm, delivers the sandwiches she has made to a fairly busy office.

Int./Ext. hairdressing salon. Fulham. Day. Montage

Helen sits in one of the chairs having her hair styled. It ends up short and blonde. Anna is standing next to her.

End of montage

Int. Anna's flat. Day

Anna and Helen. Helen is sporting her new hair style. Anna is in a bathrobe.

Helen is looking through the *Evening Standard* newspaper. She is looking for a particular page.

Anna

You don't mean that.

Helen

I do. Really.

Anna

So you were together two and a half years, you've been sitting here like suicide on a stick for a week . . .

Helen

Nine days, Anna.

Anna

. . . for nine days, but 'Bollocks to him!'

Helen

Yes. I mean, why hasn't he even called to see if I'm OK or to admit that he's a twat? 'Hello, Helen, it's Gerry, I'm a twat, please come home, I love you', all that shit. Oh, I don't care anyway. Bollocks to him. I'm over him.

Anna

Oh – you're over him?

Helen

Yes. Totally and utterly and completely over him.

Anna

No you're not.

Helen
(*continues reading*)

I am.

Anna

You're not.

Helen
(*looking up*)

Anna – I'm over him. What do you mean, I'm not? How do you know I'm not?

Anna

Well, two things really. One, you are still counting how long you've been apart in days – and probably hours and minutes – but the big flashing red light way of telling you're not really over

46

someone is when you're still reading their horoscope in the hope that they're going to get wiped out in some freak napalming incident.

Helen throws the paper at Anna.

Helen

Smart-arse!

Anna

What is he?

Helen

A wanker . . . Oh, Taurus.

Anna
(*reading*)
Taurus, Taurus – Well, just shows how much I know.
(*reads*)
'With Mars your ruler in the ascendancy you will get wiped out in a freak napalming incident and Helen says bollocks to you.' This guy's very good.

The door bell rings. They look at each other.

Helen

You go. No, I will. No you. I'm not in, I'm out. You don't know where or who with – especially who with. Quickly, go on.

Anna

I'm not answering the door like this.
(*indicates robe*)

Helen

You have to. Please. It won't be him anyway.

Anna

So, there's no big deal, is there?

Helen leaves the room.

Int. Anna's flat. Hallway. Night

Helen walks down the hall to the front door.

> **Helen**
> (*muttering*)
> Bollocks to him, bollocks to him, bollocks to him, bollocks to him . . .

She opens the door. It's James.

Cut to:

Int. American diner. Evening

James and Helen sit on bar stools with big chocolate milkshake monstrosities in front of them. James slurps the last of his. Helen plays with hers with her straw.

> **James**
> Come on. You don't drink your fatty drinks you will never really achieve quality cellulite.

Helen smirks slightly.

> Hair cut suits you, by the way.

She looks at him.

> No – it does. No gag. 'Never make a joke about women's hair, clothes or menstrual cycles' – page one. Page two: 'Don't let women know about page one.' Page three: 'Now look what you've done.'

Nothing from Helen. He looks at her with a 'Hello' face.

> **Helen**
> Listen, James, maybe I shouldn't be here. I'm sorry. I'm not being fair. You know, under normal circumstances, etc. You're really nice. And funny. And my friend Anna thinks you're cute.

James
(*feigning outrage*)
Wait, wait. Hold. Your friend Anna thinks I'm cute? Your friend
Anna thinks I'm cute? Shit, I just blew, wait –
(*picks up the menu*)
– er . . . two eighty-two eighty-five – five on the wrong girl.

Helen laughs. He takes both of her hands. Looks straight at her.

Helen. Sometimes, you know, we are plonked into people's
lives when they just need to be cheered up and reassured and it
turns out that for some reason it's your job. We don't know why.
But I'll be honest. The fact that I find you moderately attractive
does make the job easier on my part. But . . . *but* . . . that's . . .
that should not worry you at all. Well – a bit. It should worry you
a bit. But only a really little bit. No. Kidding. My intentions are
completely honourable. I have no desire to overstep the mark.
Seriously. You prefer sapphires or diamonds? Sorry! Nothing –
sorry.

Helen
Moderately attractive?

James
Ha, ha. I knew you were listening. Well, you know, lose the sad
eyes and droopy mouth and I can get you an upgrade. So,
having firmly established the ground rules, what are you doing
two weeks on Saturday?

Helen
Probably killing myself.

James
Excellent. What time does that finish? You like boats?

She looks at him.

INT. GERRY'S FLAT. LIVING ROOM. NIGHT

A TV screen shows a movie with a CLOSE SHOT of a pirate galleon crashing against the waves. Pull away to reveal the room lit by candlelight. The remnants of a home-cooked meal on the large coffee table. Helen and Gerry sit on the floor with their backs against the sofa. Helen is wearing a robe. Gerry his jockey shorts. They have a glass of wine each. There is a warm feeling. They have obviously just made love.

A Moment.

> HELEN
> You know, we haven't done that for two months?

> GERRY
> Don't be daft.

> HELEN
> Two months. Almost to the day.

> GERRY
> Almost to the day! Listen to you! What are we, a survey? We did it much more recently than – my birthday! There, we did it on my birthday . . .

> HELEN
> In May. It's July.

Gerry can't think of anything to say.

> GERRY
> May, June, Jul . . . Bloody hell.

> HELEN
> Gerry, how did one of my Waterford crystal brandy glasses get into the laundry basket?

Gerry's face.

> GERRY
> Into the where?

> HELEN
> The laundry basket.

GERRY

I don't know. Can I answer questions on 70s rock music?

HELEN

And last week, when I got the sack and I came back – am I
going mad but there was a bottle of brandy and two glasses
on the dressing table, wasn't there?

GERRY

Er, I'm sorry, I really couldn't say.

HELEN

Well, there were, I'm sure.

GERRY

No, wait a minute I could say. There, er, there – yes, there was
a bottle of brandy and one glass because if you remember I
had . . .

HELEN

No. I'm certain there were two glasses, Gerry, because I . . .

GERRY

Well, you must have imagined the second one because . . .

HELEN

I didn't though. There were tw–

GERRY

Helen, I'm not sure I like the way this conversation is going.
There was one glass. OK? One glass. I told you I couldn't
sleep and I got up in the night and got a drink to knock me
out. It was still there when you got back. You had also that
day, if you remember, taken a blow to the head. However, I
don't know how a glass wound up in the laundry basket. OK.
Sorry. We had just had a party. Maybe one of your mad
friends like Anna put it in there. I don't know. I didn't actually
see it. It's a guess. Jesus . . . I mean, let's . . . let's spoil the
moment properly, you know – Am I shagging a brandy
drinker, yes?

HELEN

Gerry, ease up, will you? I'm only asking . . . Christ's
sake . . .

GERRY

No – no you're not. Women don't ask. They never ask, they
insinuate. You are insinuating – not very subtly may I say –
that I am . . . thanks. I just can't . . . thanks. No, thank you
very much. Really, you know, I . . . I . . . This is as good a
time as any to address the state of our relationship . . . you
know . . . It's perfect. It's the perfect moment.

HELEN

Gerry, for God's sake. I asked a simple question – there's no
need to become Woody Allen.

Gerry gets up and picks up the dirty dinner plates and heads for
the kitchen.

(*to herself*)

That's it. Storm off into the kitchen. Now do angry washing
up.

The sound of the plates being dumped aggressively into the sink.

In the kitchen Gerry looks out of the window into the dark abyss
of the night.

Ext. Anna's flat. Night

James is dropping Helen off in his car. She is a little awkward. She
leans down to him in the car.

Helen

Thanks, James. I'm sorry if you had a lousy time. I'm er . . .

James

Are you kidding? In my book getting to drink two chocolate
milkshakes in one sitting represents social splendour. It's one of
the perks of being shallow. Take care, Helen. You'll be fine.

She smiles weakly and shuts the door. He pulls away. Helen waits until he is gone and then hails a cab and gets in.

Ext. Gerry's flat. Night

Helen gets out of her taxi and looks across the road at the front of the house. She goes to the door. Stands there for a second or two. She is not sure what to do.

Int. Gerry's flat. Living room. Night

Gerry is sitting with Lydia on the couch watching the pirate film. Gerry is distracted. In a world of his own.

> **Lydia**
> You OK? You seem distracted.

> **Gerry**
> (*bluffing*)
> No, I'm just thinking about the book. I'm so close. It's the bloody ending. I can't seem to relax on it.

> **Lydia**
> Ooh, I think I might be able to help you there.

She lowers her head out of shot down onto his lap. The sound of the door bell. Gerry jumps up without a word and goes to answer it.

Lydia's face. Frustrated. Is this going to work out?

Ext. Gerry's flat. Night

Helen waiting by the door. The hall light goes on.

Int. Gerry's flat. Night

Gerry walks to the front door. He opens it. There is no one there.

Ext. Gerry's flat. Night

Huddled down behind the front wall peering through a bush is

Helen. Her POV of Gerry looking around to see who rang on the bell. He goes back in.

Helen slides down on to the pavement in a disconsolate mood.

She gets up and walks away.

INT. GERRY'S FLAT. NIGHT

Helen and Gerry lie in bed together. Apart. After a moment Gerry moves his hand over to hold Helen's on top of the duvet.

> GERRY
> I'm sorry, Helen. I shouldn't have reacted like that. I'm uptight.

> HELEN
> No, someone obviously put it in there at the party. Probably Anna, you're right.

> GERRY
> I mean, you're doing all these crappy jobs to keep the money coming in, I know that. And I . . . I'm . . .

> HELEN
> I'll get another PR job.

He kisses her hand over the duvet.

> GERRY
> I know you will. I love you.

> HELEN
> Good.

She turns over. But her eyes stay open. Her mind racing. On the other side of the bed Gerry's face is in turmoil.

INT. GERRY'S FLAT. LIVING ROOM. DAY

The next day. The living room door opens and Helen comes in. Gerry is at the table writing on a piece of paper. He has his jacket on.

HELEN

It's amazing how you can actually learn to despise inanimate
objects. Like tin openers that don't open tins, egg mayonnaise
and skipjack tuna. You going out?

GERRY

Yes, I was just writing you a note. I'm off to the library.
Something I want to check up on.

Helen looks a little disappointed.

HELEN

Oh, OK.

GERRY

I won't be more than a couple of hours. Would you rather I
didn't go?

HELEN

No, no, course not. Go.

He gives her a kiss and leaves. She looks at the door thoughtfully.

CUT TO:

EXT. STREETS. DAY

Gerry walks along the road. He turns off one street into another.

A little way behind we see that Helen is following him like an old-
fashioned spy. She hides behind trees, lamp-posts and cars, so as
not to be spotted. She isn't too sure exactly what she is doing.

They go down several more streets. Finally Gerry crosses a main
road and goes up the steps and into a large building. Helen stands
there watching. The building is the library.

She suddenly feels low and not a little foolish. She wanders off
disconsolately.

INT. LIBRARY CORRIDOR. DAY

Gerry is on the payphone. He is anxious.

> GERRY
>
> Lydia, what are you talking about? She followed me!! I said I
> was going to the library, so I have come to the library, for
> God's s– Of course I can't come now. What if she comes back
> or she's waiting round the corner or something . . . Lydia, I
> don't know *why* she followed me – I'm not a sleuth. No,
> please don't – Don't get hysterical – Look, I'm sorry.

INT. LYDIA'S FLAT. DAY

Intercut with above scene.

A fed-up Lydia on the phone.

> LYDIA
>
> I've booked the hotel in Devon. Are we still going? Do you
> want me to cancel it? Is she going to follow you there? Do you
> want to end this, Gerry, because I'm not . . .

> GERRY
>
> Yes – No, I mean – no, I don't want. Of course we're still
> going. Don't . . . don't . . .

> LYDIA
>
> Don't what?

> GERRY
>
> I don't know. Look, we're going to Devon, OK? We'll have a
> . . . a great time. I'll talk to you tomorrow.

He hangs up.

Ext. James's mother's country home. Day

Establish a grand detached house in the Home Counties with
sweeping gravel drive. A car drives in the drive and up to the door.

Int. James's mother's country house. Day

James' Mother lies in bed reading a magazine. She is an elegant 70-year-old woman. She is obviously not too well.

She sits herself up and puts down her magazine in expectation. The door opens and James comes in.

James

Hello, Mum.

Mum

James!

James

Now, don't worry, the Ferrari people have been on the phone and as long as you promise to have a couple of driving lessons this week you're definitely in pole position for the Monte Carlo Grand Prix next Sunday.

He goes over and gives her a kiss.

How are you?

Mum

I'm fine.

He looks at her. She has to be honest with him.

The sale has gone through. It's going to be hard to leave this place, James, but . . .

James

But you've still got the London flat. You'll be nearer the hospital and you get much better crack in town. You know what those Monty Python boys say?

Mum

Nobody expects the Spanish Inquisition, I know.

James

Exactly. Now, as usual, there is some good news. I got the

American contract. They made one major error. They forgot to ask me if I knew what I was talking about.

Mum
Oh, James, that's great news. Your dad would have been very proud.

A moment.

James
I hope so . . . Oh and I've brought someone to see you.

He goes over to the door and opens it.

We see him lead a female hand into the room. Someone we have never met before. A woman of 32. She stands arm-in-arm with James. Mum's face lights up.

Mum
Claudia. How nice to see you, dear. How are you?

Claudia
I'm great. I'm sorry I haven't been down with James for a while, I'm just so busy at the moment.

Mum
I understand. You work hard. Give me a hug. Isn't the news great?

Claudia
Fantastic.

James
Right, well you know how adulation embarrasses me. I've got a few things to collect from the study so I'll leave you to discuss how brilliant I am in private.

He blows a kiss and leaves the room.

Int. Anna's flat. Kitchen. Day

Anna comes in. Helen looks up at her.

Anna

Right. That's the lot. You don't live there any more.

Helen

Thanks for going again, Anna. Was he there?

Anna shakes her head.

Helen

Any evidence of 'her'?

Anna

Nothing that stood out.

The phone rings. Anna goes to answer it. Helen continues to sort out her stuff. Anna calls back in.

Helen.

Int. James's mother's house. Study. Day

James keeps an eye on the door as he speaks to Helen.

James

Yes tonight tonight. You know the tonight that comes immediately after today. There'll be a gang of us. We're celebrating. The first American shipment arrived. It'll be a laugh. Please come.

Int. Anna's flat. Kitchen. Day

Anna stands egging Helen on.

Helen

Well, OK. All right.

Int. James's mother's house. Day

James

Great. See you.

James puts down the phone as Claudia comes in.

OK?

Claudia

Yeah. She doesn't really want to leave here.

He goes over and holds her.

James

I know. You're a dream, you know that, don't you?

He gives her a kiss. She looks at him fondly. She touches his face.

INT. LOCAL PUB. NIGHT

Gerry sits with Russell.

RUSSELL

Wait a sec, sorry, let me just . . . Lydia is becoming more and more demanding and you feel bad because Helen is working night and day to keep the money coming in, but you have asked Helen to come on a research trip to Devon with you knowing she would not be able to, to cover up the fact that you are taking Lydia! And, although Lydia offered you an out on the phone, which you didn't take, you are having a moral dilemma. Gerry, you are a morality-free zone. Ha ha ha!

GERRY

If I had no morals would I be discussing it? I had to ask Helen, don't you see? It's what I would do under normal circumstances. How come you don't get any of these quandaries?

RUSSELL

I've got my boxing, matey. It's up front. Honourable. Two warriors in the ring – slugging it out. Nothing underhand. All blows below the belt are immediately dealt with.

GERRY

It's barbaric.

Is it? You have spent the last two months repeatedly punching your girlfriend in the nuts and boxing is barbaric? Oh dear. I have to say that being with you makes the agonising wait before the next episode of *Seinfeld* much easier to bear. Ha ha ha. So who's idea was this trip? Yours or Lydia's?

Gerry's face answers the question.

Uhuh. You want to get out of this Lydia thing. I foresee problems. You're getting sloppy. And I wouldn't mind betting you're talking to yourself in the mirror again. Yes?

GERRY
You have no compassion. None. Why do I bother confiding in you?

RUSSELL
I'm your mate. I'm here to help you. Ha ha!

Int. restaurant. Night

Music over. Helen and James are at a table with eight of James' business colleagues, male and female. They are celebrating.

James and his mates render 'The Spanish Inquisition' sketch loudly. High-octane frivolity.

We isolate Helen to see that she is having a good time and enjoying being with James. He's on sparkling form.

Various shots of the evening. Little moments between James and Helen.

Ext. Anna's. Night

Helen and James are walking up to Anna's house.

James
I'm deadly serious.

Helen

Just set up my own PR company?

James

Why not? You've got the experience, the know-how, the contacts. You want to spend the rest of your life working for other people? Hey? What's the worst that can happen?

Helen

I could fail miserably and look like a complete tosser.

James

Exactly, so what's there to worry about?

They have arrived at the door. She smiles at him. What happens now?

Helen

I had a really nice time, James.

James

Did you? Shit, I'm sorry, that's against the rules, isn't it?

Helen

Yes, it is, so just bear that in mind in future, would you? I'm getting over a major break-up.

His face shows a fleeting glitch which he immediately masters.

James

Yes, sorry. It won't happen again.

He kisses her politely on the cheek.

Goodnight, Helen.

He walks off a few paces and turns back.

You know, everything happens for the best, Helen. You'll never know if you don't try. Take care.

He walks off. Helen looks after him. He disappears round the corner. Helen's face.

Fade to black:

Ext. street (Kelly Girl). Day

Helen is looking in the window of Kelly Girl, checking out the temp jobs. They look pretty uninspiring. She wanders off disconsolately.

Ext. bank. Day

Helen passes a bank. There is a poster in the window advertising 'Easy and Immediate' small business loans. She ponders briefly and goes in.

Cut to:

Int. Anna's flat. Living room. Day

Anna and Helen stand over application forms as Helen fills them in.

Anna
So what other ideas has James 'run by you'?

Helen
Anna. Don't do that. Don't do 'desperate mother' acting with me. He's a friend. OK? A friend. I am not remotely interested in him romantically.

Anna
You're not?

Helen
No.

Anna
So how come last night was the first night since you've been here you didn't ask if 'anyone had called' the second you walked in the door?

Helen looks up at her.

Cut to:

64

Int. Anna's kitchen. Day

Helen opens a letter from the bank. She screams with delight.

Int. small office. Day

Helen is being shown a small but neat office space by an Estate Agent.

She nods. It's fine.

    Mix to:

Int. small office. Day

Helen and Anna are up ladders painting the walls.

    Mix to:

Int. small office. Day

A carpet is being laid. Helen and Anna struggle to manoeuvre a desk through the door as an Engineer fixes in a phone line.

    Mix to:

Int. small office. Day

The office is ready. Helen sits at her desk in front of her computer playing with her new business card with Helen Quilley Public Relations written on it.

There is a bunch of flowers with a good luck card from James on the desk.

An office sandwich delivery guy knocks on the door and comes in with a basket of sandwiches and a card. He is touting for business.

INT. LONDON OFFICE. DAY

Helen stands with her sandwich basket on her arm. She is very

weary, having held down both jobs for a good while. She is being berated by an extremely unhappy and abusive Customer. We can only see Helen at this point.

                    IRATE CUSTOMER
                      (*voice-over*)
Well, I'm afraid that is little use to me, is it?

                        HELEN
I suppose not.

                    IRATE CUSTOMER
                      (*voice-over*)
You suppose not. You only suppose not.

                        HELEN
No, I mean . . . yes, of course. I'm sorry.

As the camera moves round in front of the desk we see that the irate customer is in fact Lydia.

                        LYDIA
You're sorry. You're sorry that four of the staff here have been cut down with food poisoning after eating your sandwiches. And before you speak, yes they all had the same sandwiches and the same symptoms at the same time. Are you trained in the catering trade, may I ask?

                        HELEN
No, I actually work in PR but I er . . .

                        LYDIA
Well, you are not doing a particularly good PR job this morning, are you? Luckily for you I have convinced my colleagues not to take the matter any further. This time. Now, if you will excuse me, I have five people's work to do.

Helen leaves the room shell-shocked.

INT. LYDIA'S OFFICE. HALLWAY. DAY

Helen walks disconsolately to the lift and presses the button. She puts down her basket and leans her head against the wall. She begins to sob.

CUT TO:

INT. BERTORELLI'S. EVENING

Helen at work at the bistro. She is quite distracted – almost in a trance with fatigue and the memory of the horrible events of the morning.

She plonks some dirty plates in the kitchen and picks up the pay phone and dials.

CUT TO:

INT. GERRY'S FLAT. EVENING

The phone rings and the answerphone clicks on.

CUT TO:

INT. BERTORELLI'S. EVENING

Helen tuts and puts the phone down. She gets out her Filofax from her bag. Picks up the phone to dial again.

INT. LYDIA'S FLAT. LIVING ROOM. EVENING

Lydia and Gerry are sitting on her sofa.

GERRY
Sorry – Helen came to your office today?!

LYDIA
Yes. I had reason to summon her. Well, I made up a reason to summon her to be brutally honest. She's quite pretty in an average Home Counties sort of way, isn't she?

68

GERRY

Lydia! What are you playing at? Have you gone raving mad?
She's not bloody stupid, you know.

LYDIA

Ooh, I wouldn't say that. I wanted to see what the woman
you ditched me for is like.

GERRY

Wait a sec . . . I did not ditch you for . . . you went back to
America for Chr– Lydia where is your head with thi–

LYDIA

I wanted to see what this girl you seem to have no intention of
leaving – despite the occasional pre-orgasmic suggestion that
you are – had that was so . . . unleavable. And I have to say I
ended our brief meeting at a bit of a loss.

GERRY

Don't talk like this, Lydia, it sounds ugly. I've told you – I
can't leave Helen for . . . for . . . you know . . .

LYDIA

For me? Is that what you were going to say? You can't leave
her for me?

GERRY

You've never said you wanted that, have you?

LYDIA

Gerry – I'm a woman. We don't say what we want. But we
still reserve the right to be pissed off if we don't get it. It's
what makes us so fascinating. And not a little scary. You have
to go. Helen will be wondering where you are.

She kisses him maternally. He is dismissed.

CUT TO:

INT. GERRY'S BEDROOM. NIGHT

Gerry sits on the bed in a dilemma. The phone rings at the same time as the key goes in the front door. He answers the phone.

> GERRY

Hello.

> RUSSELL
> (*voice-over*)

At last. It's Russell, listen, wherever you were tonight, as if we need to ask, you weren't with me. Helen called looking for you.

> GERRY

Thanks.

He hangs up. Helen comes in.

Thank God. I was worried. Where've you been?

> HELEN

I went to Anna's. I needed to see a friendly face. I've had a horrible day. I met Cruella de Ville's less nice sister this morning and she completely deflated me.

> GERRY

I know.

> HELEN

How do you know?

He goes over to her, thinking on his feet.

> GERRY

No, I mean I can tell, you look worn out.

> HELEN

Where were you earlier? I really needed to talk to you.

> GERRY

I'm sorry, I went to the library to read up on some stuff. Come here. Take off that coat. Here.

He lays her down on the bed and begins to stroke her forehead. He looks at her really fondly.

HELEN

You practically live at that library. Oh God, I'm sick of waiting on tables. I know when you finish the book we'll be millionaires but . . . Will you be much longer? When are you going to finish it?

GERRY

I'm going to finish it very soon. Very soon. I really love you, Helen.

He holds her really tight to him.

Tight on Gerry. His face shows some kind of decision taking place. After a moment.

Helen, I've got something I want to tell you. I need to tell you. It's um . . . Well it's a bit to do with the brandy glass and, er . . . a bit to do with the woman you met today . . . only please let me finish before you say anything, OK? Helen? Helen.

He leans over to see her face. She is fast asleep.

GERRY
(*defeatedly*)

Bollocks.

FADE TO BLACK:

Ext. Thames Embankment at Hammersmith. Day

A long rowing boat comes towards the camera out of a shed.

It is put into the water by the crew. One of them is James. Clive is on the team as well.

Helen is watching. She is wearing a jumper and jacket. She holds up two crossed fingers to James.

Cut to:

Ext. River Thames. Day

The race in progress. James and his seven other team members giving it all they've got against the other crew. It is very close.

Helen is on a small support launch following by the side. She is willing James on in a conservative manner.

The race goes under Putney Bridge. As it does we pan up to the bridge to find:

EXT. PUTNEY BRIDGE. DAY

Helen walking along the road with Anna. Helen looks out over the river to see the boat race going past. James and Clive rowing away energetically. (N.B. **Helen** is not on the support launch.)

> HELEN
> That's really weird. I knew there would be a boat race going by with blue and yellow shirts. Sorry?

> ANNA
> How come he hasn't asked you to go with him to Devon?

> HELEN
> He has. I have to work. Anyway it'll be good for him to get away. He's been slogging hard on the book. He needs the space. I suppose we both do. Anna, can I ask you a daft question? Did you drop a glass in the laundry basket at our party?

> ANNA
> Sounds like a ridiculous thing to do. It was almost certainly me. Are you OK?

> HELEN
> I'm just going quietly mad.

> ANNA
> Thank God. I was worried.

72

They wander off.

CUT TO:

Ext. River Thames. Day

The race gathers momentum as they reach the final stages.

Helen becomes more and more vociferous until she is screaming and jumping up and down in excitement.

James' team crosses the line just ahead of the others. Helen is ecstatic.

Cut to:

Int. Boat Club Bar. Day

A full clubhouse bar. Everybody is singing 'Father Abraham has seven sons', a high-action energetic drinking song, led by James who stands on a table at the front. Clive is there too.

Helen is trying to keep up with all the various actions and is having a great time.

Cut to:

Ext. Boat Club. Embankment. Day

Along the Embankment come Gerry and Lydia.

Lydia
Darling, it's just writer's block. You'll be OK.

Gerry glances in the window of the club and sees the frivolity inside. Helen is jumping up and down, throwing her arms and legs out as the song requires.

Gerry
That's Helen in there. She's got blonde hair.

He goes over to the window and peers in. Lydia keeps walking.

There's loads of them having some kind of sponsored epileptic fit.

He sees that Lydia has moved on.

Lydia!

She spins round viciously.

Lydia
Maybe it isn't writer's block at all, Gerry. Maybe it's Helen block. Allow me to talk to you in a condescending fashion. I – don't – want – to – hear – about – Helen, Gerry. I – don't – care – about – Helen. Understand? The trouble is, you do. Quite clearly. So, call me when you've decided which one of us you want.

She storms off.

Gerry
Lydia . . . I . . . tchoh Jesus.

He looks on. This relationship is not going to work.

Int. Boat Club bar. Day (golden hour)

Helen stands at the bar with James and Clive.

James
Yes, you are, Clive. See what I mean? He's too modest. He is one of the most naturally gifted chefs around. But of course being talented he's totally weird and unpredictable. He's opening his first restaurant in six days but he 'doesn't want a big affair'. Typical genius, he's completely barking.

Helen
Well, not everyone wants the big hype. At my old company we had wars getting Pierre Claude to let us do his launch.

Clive
You did Pierre Claude? Oh shit, he's my hero. I did a couple of his master classes. He's so free and reckless. You did his

launch? I heard that was a really classy do. People went on about it.

Helen
Well, it hasn't done him any harm, certainly. He opens in New York and Beverly Hills next month.

Clive
I heard, yeah.

Helen
Can I come and look at your place? I mean six days is . . . I can't promise anything stupendous but . . .

Clive
Sure yeah, no problem. You kidding? Come down. It's a bit of a tip still but . . . we're getting there. I'll cook you some lunch. Wow. Shit man, Pierre Claude, that really is like huge amounts of 'wow', James, you know.

James
So it would seem.

Helen gives him a card. James smiles. Clive is happy.

Mix to:

Ext. on the River Thames. Night

Helen and James are in a rowing boat near Albert Bridge. James is rowing. There is an unmistakable warm feeling. They stop and look out over the river.

Helen
Thanks for that.

He looks at her.

Clive.

James
He really is top-notch. Just needs someone on the reins.

76

Helen

You're very thoughtful, James. You give out an incredible amount.

James

You're the same, you encouraged me today. I could see you jumping up and down like a mad thing during the race. Spurred me on.

She looks a tad embarrassed. Cups her nose to hide her face.

Helen

Aren't you a bit old for that kind of exertion?

James

Aren't you a bit close to water for that kind of question?

Helen

I love this bridge. My great grandfather helped to build it. I often come and stand on it when I want to . . . er . . .

James

Build a bridge? Sorry.

She gets up to punch his arm. They topple slightly. He grabs her. Their faces are close. They look at each other. He goes to kiss her. She stops him.

Helen

No, please, James. Don't. Oh God, I'm sorry, I mean I . . . I know this is a pretty ideal sort of kissing moment. Night, moon, boat, water lapping, you know, I . . . It's perfect – and I'm not not feeling that it would be nice because you're nice and . . . and – crap word, I know, but you are, you're really really nice – and, and the whole day has been just so . . .

James

Nice?

She giggles.

Helen

Yes, yes it has. It's been perfect. I've had a great time. You've given me so much in such a short space of time.

James

So have you.

Helen

But, I don't know anything about you. And I'm still on the 'rebound' – urgh, I hate that word – but I am.

James

Who isn't? Everyone is. We spend our whole lives on the rebound. All of us. We bounce happily from one dilemma to the next. I'm on the rebound myself in . . . in a way, er . . .

It seems like he could launch into something quite deep.

The moment changes slightly.

Helen

You OK?

James
(*recovering*)

Yeah. Yeah.

Helen

So who are you on the rebound from?

James

A girl called Pamela. Yes, everything in my life pivots round Pam and I breaking up.

Helen

How long ago was that?

James

Nineteen seventy-three. We were eight. I bloody loved that woman.

Helen laughs.

No warning. Just gone. Left me for someone else.

Helen

Who?

James

Gary Glitter.

Helen

The cow.

James

Gary Glitter, for crying out loud!! I mean, all my pals were being left for Donny Osmond or David Cassidy. I could have somehow come to terms with that given time. But Gary. She wanted to 'touch him there, yeah', you know. Well, I went to pieces, as you can imagine. And there was no Junior Prozac to help me through so . . .

Helen suddenly kisses him hard but quick and solidly. She pulls away. They look at each other.

A long moment.

Er . . . so um . . . I . . . it . . .

Helen

I kissed you.

James

Yes, I spotted that too. You weren't going to do that.

Helen

I know. I know. Er . . . would you er . . . I mean would you mind putting it down to a momentary lapse of concentration?

James

Is that what it was?

Helen

No. Yes. I don't . . . oh help.

He takes her by the shoulders and looks at her hard.

James

I don't want to be a confusion in your life, Helen. I don't. Truly. But *something* has happened to me since I met you that I . . . I wasn't expecting. Didn't really, er . . . well, wasn't expecting. Oh oh, repetition of expecting. Must buy a thesaurus. Anyway . . . er . . .

He suddenly seems very open and vulnerable.

Helen puts her finger tenderly over his lips. They stare intently at each other. She caresses his face tenderly with the back of her hand.

Mix to:

Int. Anna's flat. Night

Silhouette. James and Helen are making love. It is beautiful.

Mix to:

Int. Anna's flat. Day

Helen wakes up and looks to the pillow next to her. James has gone. She looks around but there is a note on the pillow. It says: 'Now that's what I call a BIG lapse of concentration! Didn't want to wake you or embarrass your friend. James x'.

She smiles at the note and stares into the middle distance thoughtfully.

Fade to blackout

EXT. GERRY'S FLAT. DAY

Lydia's car is parked right outside the front of the flat. The boot is open and she is standing by the open driver's door, honking the horn casually.

Gerry comes out quickly and nervously. He has one little bag and his typewriter.

> GERRY
> You did remember to take the full page ad in *Adulterer's Weekly*?! Jesus.

She has stopped honking. Gerry puts his bag and typewriter in the boot, where we see three huge bags belonging to Lydia.

> We're going to Devon for the weekend not the rest of our lives. Quickly, come on.

He gets in the car.

Lydia stands there looking up at the front of the flat.

Gerry leans across and talks to her through the open driver's door.

> Lydia, come on. Get in, will you!

> LYDIA
> How many years have you been going to paint that stain off?

She gets in calmly and drives off.

INT. BERTORELLI'S. DAY

Helen is dashing from table to table. The place is really busy. There is a band playing in the corner.

She goes to a table. A cheeky bloke tries a chat-up job on her.

> CHEEKY BLOKE
> Hey, gorgeous. What do you do when you're not serving up mad cow burgers in here?

> HELEN
> (*skilfully dismissive*)
> Well, now then, let me see. I get up about 7.30 a.m., make and deliver sandwiches in the West End during the day, before I come here at about 6 o'clock, and finish at midnight.

81

And then when I leave here at night I go home and wash my hair, which you can imagine is quite smelly by then. Er . . . after that if I've got any energy left I give my boyfriend a blow job, something which, though I say it myself and shouldn't, I'm pretty nifty at. Would you like some mayonnaise with that?

CUT TO:

EXT. DEVON HOTEL. DAY

High establishing shot of the plush country hotel. Lydia's car pulls up outside.

INT. BERTORELLI'S. EVENING

Helen works away at the restaurant. It's as busy as ever. She looks weary and a little distracted.

(VISUAL NOTE: This sequence of Helen working hard and getting more and more dizzy and nauseous will intermix over the next scenes. It will show that at this stage of the story in one 'life' Helen is working merely as a waitress in a restaurant and that in the other 'life' Helen in her PR capacity is masterminding the opening of a high-class restaurant. Shots of Helen gradually become slow motion until she finally stumbles, dropping plates all over the floor.)

Int. Clive's restaurant. Night

Champagne is poured into a glass.

Pull wide. The opening-night party is in full swing.

The restaurant has been done up beautifully. Helen has done a great job. There are representatives from every top magazine there, celebrities, gliterati. Photographers snap away.

The food being passed around looks absolutely sumptuous. The banter is high and positive. Helen looks radiant. James looks on proudly and Clive can hardly contain himself. We move around the party from group to group.

At one moment Helen is chatting to a group of people including James and Clive and some Catering Journalists. She looks around to see how things are going in the rest of the room and her gaze falls full on:

Gerry!

He is staring at her. She immediately loses all her cool. James sees that she has plainly seen something that has thrown her . . . He sees Gerry, realising from her reaction who it must be.

Helen blusters, heart racing.

Helen
Er . . . sorry, excuse me . . . er, for a minute. I just er . . . sorry . . . 'scuse me . . . sorry.

Cut to:

Helen and Gerry stand to one side of the room.

What do you mean you wanted to see me? Jesus Christ, Gerry, what . . . how did you get in?

Gerry
One of the waiters is a friend of Russell's. Got me a ticket. It's a great do, Helen. I hear you're really taking off with your company. I'm thril–

Helen
Gerry, you can't just . . . just *turn up* like this. This is a big night for me. Look at me, I've gone all clammy.

Gerry is very focused and sincere.

Gerry
Yes, I can, Helen. I can 'just turn up' – I had to 'just turn up'. Don't you see, this is the most important 'just turn up' I've ever done. I want you to have clammy hands. I . . .

Helen is aware that this is not the place to have this conversation.

Helen

We can't talk in here.

Cut to:

Ext. Clive's restaurant. Night

Helen and Gerry stand outside the restaurant. Through the window in the background the festivities continue. They look and sound like a dull blur.

Gerry

Helen, we have been through too much to just drop this. Haven't we? Surely. If I've embarrassed you tonight I'm really sorry, but if I've embarrassed myself then I don't care. I don't care how much of a fool I look as long as you can see how much I don't want to lose you.

Helen

Gerry . . .

Gerry

The fact is this, Helen. If I end up looking like a complete twat and I still don't get you back, then as long as you listened to me and could see how much this means to me – you mean to me – then I don't give a toss how I look to the rest of the world. Helen, look at me – I'm sorry. Really sorry. You are too important not to fight for. And I'll fight. Even if I lose. I'll fight to the last.

Helen

Gerry, don't talk about fight . . . Oohh! God! I'm . . . Gerry . . .

Helen looks a little lost. Gerry has disarmed her slightly. She looks around, a little unsure of what to do or say. Her gaze takes in the party through the window. She sees James staring out at them.

James has sensed her reaction to seeing Gerry. Gerry turns round to

84

see what she is looking at. James and Gerry are briefly eye to eye.

Gerry

Good-looking bloke. Are you seeing him?

Helen

Uh, he . . . look.

Gerry

No, I can't ask that, I'm sorry. It's not my place.

Int. Clive's restaurant. Night

James stands looking at Helen and Gerry. Clive appears at his shoulder.

Clive

Is that him?

James

I guess so.

Clive

Have you told her about Claudia?

James

No, not yet. But you know. It's a tricky one. I'll tell her all my secrets when the time is right. There's no rush. I really like her, Clive. Do you think she still has feelings for him? I'm confused. I feel a bit lost suddenly.

Clive

Good.

James

Good?

Clive

Yeah. You're always so together and witty and charming and in control and unphasable and, to be quite frank, you get on my bloody tits!

They laugh. Clive has helped.

Ext. Clive's restaurant. Night

Helen
Gerry, I have to go back inside. You know . . .

Gerry
Will you come and see me, Helen? Please. There's so much more I want to say.

Helen
I don't know. Uh, God, why is everything so complicated.

Gerry
It doesn't have to be. I miss you. Do you miss me?

Helen
Don't ask me that, Gerry. Please go. Please. This is a really important night.

Gerry
Do you? Will you come and see me? Helen?

She looks at him. She is slightly in turmoil.

Well, I'll go. Thanks for listening. Have a good night. I'm really proud of you.

He kisses her hard on the lips and leaves her frozen on the spot. He walks off.

Helen stands for a moment. She looks in through the window of the restaurant. James has seen the kiss. He is looking at her. He looks a little dazed.

She starts to move off and stumbles in a slight faint. A Guest leaving the party catches her.

Guest
You OK?

Helen

Yes, thank you. Just went a bit dizzy. Too much champagne.

(Important visual note: This dizzy faint will coincide with Helen stumbling in the restaurant as explained earlier.)

Mix to:

Int. Clive's restaurant. Night

Helen mingles through the crowded room looking for James. She goes into the kitchen to look, where she meets Clive. He wraps her up in a mad embrace.

Clive

It's official. I'm in love with you. Thank you. You're a genius. I'm ecstatic.

Helen

Have you seen James?

Clive

He had to go. Early start. He apologised. He's very taken with you, you know.

Helen

Yes, I know. Congratulations, Clive. You're a success.

They toast each other with champagne. Helen looks concerned.

Mix to:

INT. HOTEL BEDROOM. DEVON. NIGHT

Two champagne glasses clink together. Lydia and Gerry in bed.

Lydia pours champagne over Gerry's body and disappears out of shot to lick it off.

Gerry's face in torment.

MOMENTARY SPLIT MIX WITH:

INT. GERRY'S FLAT. NIGHT

Helen alone in bed. Lonely. A tear runs down her face.

FADE TO BLACK:

Int. James's mother's London flat. Day

James is settling his mother in to her flat. She is a little more frail than before. She is in a wheelchair with a rug over her.

Claudia is helping unpack boxes. James seems somewhat sullen – preoccupied.

Mum is taking smaller items out of a box by her wheelchair. Ornaments, photos, etc.

Mum
It's smaller than I remember. I haven't been here for so long. It's cosy though.

James
Course it is. Listen, Mum, I have to get back to the office, so, just call if you need anything.

He kisses her. Claudia does too.

They leave the flat. Claudia stops James in the corridor.

Claudia
Do you want to tell me what's bothering you or is it private?

He looks at her and pulls a grimace.

James
I think it's probably private, just for now.

Claudia
Well, I'm here if you need me.

James
I know. Thanks.

He touches her face.

> I have to go away for a few days.

Helen
(*voice-over*)

Business trip.

Cut to:

Int. Anna's flat. Kitchen. Evening

Helen and Anna are making a cake.

Helen
Newcastle or something. I didn't want to pry. His secretary wasn't very forthcoming.

Anna
Do you believe he's away?

Helen
Don't know.

Anna
Or do you think he's just avoiding you?

Helen
Don't know.

Anna
Did you leave a message?

Helen
No.

Anna
Do you think maybe you should have? Did he actually see Gerry kiss you?

Helen
Don't know.

Anna

Do you think he might be hoping you've called and not knowing that you have? Did you not check if he has a mobile?

Helen

Anna! Ease up, will you? Bloody hell, they have less questions than this on *Jeopardy*. I was nervous. I wanted to get off the phone. I felt awkward.

Anna

Well, it's such a piddly little thing. Hardly worth him getting uptight about. Oh, Gerry called, by the way.

Helen

Hoh, terrific. That's just . . . Two months ago I want Gerry to come round – James comes round. Now I want James to call – Gerry calls. You think if I try to really not want to win the Lottery, I will?

Anna
(*deadpan*)

No. Doesn't work like that.

They burst out laughing.

Helen

You mad sod. Stop trying to cheer me up will, you?

Anna

Sorry.

Int. Newcastle hotel bedroom. Evening

James sits on the corner of the bed with his jacket off and tie undone. He has the hotel notepad on his lap and has scribbled lots of notes on it.

He picks up the phone to dial. He dials a few numbers and then disconnects with his finger. He takes his finger off and stares at the dial as if he were being dared to brave a lion's den.

He hangs up. Stands up and walks around the room looking at his notes. He looks at the phone from across the room.

Int. Anna's flat. Kitchen. Evening

The phone rings. They look at each other. Anna gestures does Helen want to get it. She shakes her head manically.

Anna picks up the phone.

Anna
(*tentatively*)

Hello. Oh hello.

(*eyes to Helen*)

Yes. Yes she's here. Would you like to talk to her? Yes. Just one second, I'll call her.

(*cups the phone*)

Helen! Phone call!

Helen has been trying to prise out of her who it is – mouths 'Who is it? Gerry? James?' – Anna offers the phone to Helen. Helen walks over nervously, still making frantic interrogative gestures. She takes the phone and composes herself for a second.

Helen

Hello.

(*to Anna*)

Oh!! You horrible evil . . . !

(*into phone*)

No, sorry, Mum . . . hang . . .

(*cups phone*)

You are evil, I hate you. With all of my heart.

Anna runs out of the room screaming with laughter.

Cut to:

EXT. HOTEL. DEVON. EARLY EVENING

Re-establish the Devon hotel.

INT. HOTEL BEDROOM. DEVON. EARLY EVENING

Gerry is on the phone to Helen. From the bathroom we can hear a bath running.

INTERCUT WITH:

INT. GERRY'S FLAT. EARLY EVENING

Helen is lying on the bed talking on the phone to Gerry.

HELEN

. . . It was the weirdest dream. I was this big success. Everyone was there, pop stars and celebrities. And there was this bloke that was trying to get off with me. Or something, you know, he was . . . and he . . . there was . . . like there was a cloud in front of him . . . or, or . . . or . . . and I couldn't really see him . . . and . . . and then you were suddenly there and the whole place was suddenly empty and we were talking but you had a funny mask on your face like you weren't really you. You had something you needed to tell me, but you couldn't say it.

GERRY

Well, that does it, I'm afraid, I'm taking away your class one drugs for a week.

HELEN

Anyway, there's something else I wanted to tell you. I fainted at work the other night.

GERRY

Oh, sweetheart. Are you OK?

HELEN

Yes, but I don't normally faint so I . . .

Sudden screeches and yelps of pain from Lydia in the bathroom. Gerry instinctively holds his hand over the mouthpiece.

What was that noise?

GERRY

I don't know, the people in the next room are plainly engaged in some bizarre sexual ritual. I might pop in and introduce myself later. What did you say?

HELEN

Well, I don't normally faint so I was a little curious . . .

But Lydia is in the room hopping up and down holding her foot in pain.

LYDIA

Ow, shit, dammit! I stubbed my foot on the side of the shagging bath. Ahhhhhhhh! Ow, ow, bollocks.

Gerry is frantically trying to get her to shush as silently as he can, pointing manically at the phone and holding his hand over the mouthpiece.

GERRY
(*mouthing only*)

Shut up – shut up!

HELEN

Sounds horrific.

GERRY

I know . . . er . . . I –

HELEN

Anyway, I was a little curious so I . . .

He knocks his knuckles twice on the side of the bed.

GERRY

Oh, look, that's room service with my sandwich – I'll call you back when world war twelve has stopped for tea.

He hangs up.

Helen is left holding a receiver with no one at the other end.

She moves the receiver away from her face a little. She speaks calmly and quietly to herself, almost trance-like.

HELEN

. . . so I did a test and it turns out that I'm pregnant. I just thought you might like to know.

She hangs up resignedly and stares into the middle distance.

INT. DEVON HOTEL BEDROOM. EARLY EVENING

Gerry has hung up the phone and is furiously berating Lydia who is sat on a chair administering to her foot.

GERRY

Are you completely insane?! What are you trying to do?

LYDIA

What do you mean, what am I trying to do? I think I've broken my toe.

GERRY

Lydia, I was on the pissing phone to Helen, for goodness' sake.

LYDIA

So?

GERRY

Sooooo! In case you had forgotten, she doesn't know you are here, she thinks that I am on a research trip – alone – remember?

LYDIA

Yeah, I remember. Don't worry, I remember. It's pretty hard to forget.

GERRY

So, what are you trying to do, coming in screeching the place down when I'm on the ph–

She leaps up at him. And as she bawls at him she limps around the room stuffing her things into her going away bag.

> LYDIA
>
> Don't you know, Gerry? Don't you know what I'm trying to do?!! I'm trying to be your girlfriend, Gerry. I'm trying to win you back. It's fairly simple. I'm standing on the platform at Limbo Central with my heart and soul packed in my suitcase waiting for the Gerry fucking Express to roll in and tell me that my ticket is still valid and that I may reboard the train. Only the station announcer keeps coming on telling me that the train has been delayed as the driver has suffered a major panic attack at Indecision City, we suggest you take the bus! That's what I'm trying to do, you cripple! Except it's fairly clear now that that is never going to happen. Is it? No reply, perfect. So I'm not waiting any more, Gerry. I'm cashing my ticket in. I'm taking that bus. I tell all my friends 'Never go back.' Look at me, I must be crazy. Don't phone me for a while. No, don't phone me at all. Ever. It's over. Again!

She storms out of the room and slams the door.

INT. BERTORELLI'S. EVENING

Various shots of Helen working away, taking orders, delivering food, mopping up spilt drinks, taking back food from unhappy customers etc., etc. She seems completely deflated and uncentred.

At one table a Couple are having a 'domestic'. Helen can't help overhearing as she clears the table next to it.

> SUSPICIOUS GIRL
>
> Because you never buy me flowers when you're meant to, let alone when you're not meant to, so yes, that's why I'm a little suspicious. I want to know what else you're doing that you're not meant to.

DEFENSIVE BLOKE

Wait, hang on. Let me get this straight, because this is just about brilliant! I buy you flowers on a whim in a . . . a . . . a fit of . . . of . . . er . . . romance . . . and . . . yet . . .

SUSPICIOUS GIRL

See, you couldn't even think of the word!

DEFENSIVE BLOKE

But instead of being grateful, instead of being *romanced*, you are instantly convinced that I must be ensconced in some decrepit, tacky, underhand, clandestine affair?

SUSPICIOUS GIRL

In a nutshell!

Helen has logged all this. She moves off with the plates.

CUT TO:

INT. LOCAL PUB. NIGHT

Gerry comes in. He is energetic.

GERRY

I've done it, Russell. I've bloody done it.

RUSSELL

Excellent. Congratulations. Done what?

GERRY

I finished it.

RUSSELL

The book! Oh well, that's great . . .

GERRY

Not the book, not the book, Russell. I'm a novelist, I'm never going to finish the book. The affair! The affair. The sordid affair. With Lydia. It's over. I've blown her out. In Devon. I was decisive but fair. I've just got back. I feel like I got out of jail. No more deceit, no more lying to Helen. It was such a mistake. Never go back Russell. But it's over. Whoo! I can't tell you, it is such a good feeling.

RUSSELL

Well, I'm very pleased. And how does she feel about it? Lydia.

GERRY

Sheee . . . she . . . well, you know, she's not jumping through hoops obviously. But it's the best thing. By far. Far and away the best thing. She knows that – well, she will do, when she's . . . I mean . . . she was upset . . . and a bit, fraught, you know, obviously. I mean, she can be a bit fraught. But she'll realise in time. It's the best thing. I have to say she was becoming very . . . odd.

RUSSELL

Odd?

GERRY

Well, she is odd. I mean she's not becoming odd, I think she has always been . . . er . . . odd. Very strange girl . . . you know . . . I came to realise. Very . . . er . . . very unsettled . . . um . . . you know.

RUSSELL

In an odd sort of way.

GERRY

God, I feel good. Look I want to be at home when Helen gets back from work. See you.

Gerry picks up his bag and leaves.

INT. GERRY'S FLAT. NIGHT

Helen comes into the flat. The living room light is on. She calls out.

HELEN

Gerry? You back?

99

GERRY
(*voice-over*)

In here.

She goes into the living room.

A glass of champagne is thrust under her nose. Gerry appears with his glass and chinks hers. He kisses her. He is hyper.

I missed you so I came home early.

Helen is suddenly in a daze. All she can think of is what happened in the restaurant.

Aren't you pleased to see me?

Helen looks over to the table and sees the flowers. It's like she has seen a ghost.

HELEN
What are they?!

GERRY
They're flowers. For you. I saw them at the station and bought them. Don't you like them?

HELEN
Er . . .

GERRY
Darling, are you OK? I thought you'd be pleased to see me.

HELEN
Er, look if you don't mind I'm going to bed. I had a really bad day.

GERRY
Hey, me coming back hasn't thrown you, has it? Not expecting your boyfriend any minute?

She can't bring herself to speak.

Darling, it's a joke.

He goes to her and holds her.

I really thought you'd be glad to see me.

She responds to his hug, but we can see from her face the feeling hasn't left her. It's an effort.

HELEN
I am. Course I am. Sorry. I'm just really tired. I'll be all right tomorrow.

GERRY
OK, darling. You're working so hard. You get some sleep. Breakfast in bed tomorrow for you.

Helen's face.

Int. Gerry's flat. Living room. Night

Helen sits on the couch. Gerry is stroking her hair.

Helen
I can't get her out of my mind. That image of her sitting on top of y . . . tch. I really don't know why I agreed to come. Look at me – what are you doing? Stop it, please. Don't do that. I don't want you to touch me, Gerry.

She gets up. Moves to the door. Picks up her coat.

Gerry
I'm sorry. Don't go. I was just being affectionate. Helen, please try to get her out of your mind. She's out of mine. It's over. Finished. It wasn't anything anyway and whatever it was it's over. It was a mistake. I made a mistake. Such a big, big mistake. I'm sorry. I'm truly, truly sorry. If I could have only seen the upset it was going to cause then . . .

Helen
Yes, well, where is retrospect when you really need it, hey?

Gerry

I mean this . . . this new bloke James Hammerton you're seeing, you know, does he not make mistakes? Is he so pristine, huh?

Helen

How do you know his name?

Gerry

I . . . found out. Accidentally. Russell's mate at the restaurant. They have mutual friends or, or . . . whatever. I don't know, look that's not especially important is it, how I know.

She becomes slightly thoughtful.

Helen

Well, I don't want to talk James Hammerton. Or anyone else. I have to go.

Gerry

I've stopped writing my book, by the way.

Helen can't help being immediately concerned.

Helen

What? Gerry! . . . You . . . you're so close to the end, you can't just stop.

Gerry

I've had to get a job at Russell's local. I need the money. Can't write and starve. They don't go together. It's no big deal.

Helen

It is a big deal. You have to finish it, Gerry, it's . . .

Gerry

Helen! The truth is I can't write without you. I can't do anything without you. I've even forgotten how to . . . brush my teeth without you! I want you to come back to me. We are so good together. Remember how good we are. We have the same sens–

The phone by the bed rings. He picks it up.

Int. Lydia's flat. Night

Lydia on the phone.

Lydia

I'm late, Gerry. Four days. I'm never late.

Int. Gerry's flat. Living room. Evening

Gerry
(*bluffing*)

Hello, Russ. Listen, mate, can I call you back in a minute? Yeah OK.

He puts down the phone. To Helen.

Russell. Dying for the loo.

He goes into the bathroom. Helen is curious and picks up the phone. She hesitates for a moment then dials 1471.

Telephone Announcer
(*voice-over*)

Telephone number 0171–444–3184 called at 6.43 p.m. To return the call press three.

She presses 3 on the phone. The phone rings. Lydia answers. She launches straight in.

Intercut with:

Int. Lydia's flat. Evening

Lydia

Why are you pretending I'm Russell, Gerry? Who have you got there? Gerry, answer me. Who's there?

Int. Gerry's flat. Living room. Evening

Helen

It's Helen actually. We met once. I interrupted you faking your orgasm. Sorry I can't be more specific.

She lays the phone on the bed. She puts on her coat and walks to the door. Lydia still chirps down the line.

Gerry comes back from the loo.

Gerry

I've just been thinking and . . .

He hears Lydia's voice still ranting away and sees the phone on the bed. It all dawns on him simultaneously. He stares helplessly at Helen. She turns wearily and looks at him. She talks finally and calmly.

Helen

You wanker. You sad, sad wanker.

She walks out. Lydia's voice continues to bark out 'Gerry! Gerry! Gerry!!'

Cut to:

Int. Anna's flat. Living room. Night

Helen is pacing up and down furiously.

Helen

God, I feel like such a mug! The useless . . . no-good, shagging, horrible, despicable, no-good two-faced, lying, pissing, shagging . . .

Anna

You said shagging.

Helen

Wanker . . . You know the worst bit? All I could think about was James. I felt like I was being unfaithful to him just being there.

Anna

That sounds like the best bit. And you were.

Helen

He didn't call, did he?

Anna shakes her head.

That's nearly a week. I think I've blown it. I've blown it, haven't I?

Anna looks at her.

Mix to:

Int. local pub. Night

Gerry sits opposite Russell.

Russell

I blame British Telecom. All this new technology. This number if you want to know who rang – another if you don't want them to know you rang – itemised bills – take away the number you first thought of – they are single-handedly condemning the average red-blooded Briton to a life of terminal monogamy. What are they after, the Nobel Peace Prize!?

Gerry

And Lydia might be pregnant.

Russell howls with laughter.

Russell

No more, please. I can't take it. Oh dear, this is terrific stuff. I must say, you do make the wait for the next series of *Seinfeld* much easier to bear.

Gerry

I didn't reckon on things ending up like this. The whole thing's a complete cock-up. What's going on?

Russell

Well, to use boxing parlance, if I may, it's quite simple. You just lost!

Gerry stands up. His mind suddenly racing.

Gerry

I'm going to get her back.

Russell

Which one? Ha ha. Sorry. How?

Gerry

I don't know. I'm going to check out the gen on this Hammerton guy. He must have some pimply imperfection. No one's perfect. Will you help me?

Russell

Gerry, you sound completely ridiculous.
(*mimics with an American accent*)
'I'm going to check out the gen on this Hammerton guy – see if I can't nail the son of a bitch, God dammit!' Ha ha!

Gerry

Listen, Russell, you want to help me or you want to take the piss out of me?

Russell

(*American accent again*)
Boy that's a tough one, Bob, but I'm going to have to go with choice 'two'.
(*English*)
Relax, will you – of course I'll help. What have you got in mind?

As Gerry is leaving he shrugs.

Gerry

I don't know.

And he's gone.

Russell

Crikey, once you set your sights on something you just become Inspirationman. Ha ha ha.

He goes back to his magazine.

INT. GERRY'S FLAT. KITCHEN. DAY

Gerry comes into the kitchen. Helen follows him in. She fills up the kettle with water and takes it over to plug it in. He gets out the milk and two mugs.

GERRY

Are you sure? You've been a bit, I don't know – distant, since I got back.

HELEN

I know. Well, OK. There are a couple of things. Which one do you want to hear first?

GERRY

Don't mind.

HELEN

Well the 'small' news is that I've got an interview for a job. A PR job. A proper one. International company opening up in London. The chairman herself called. Said she had heard a lot about me and she's invited me to her apartment for a 'serious chat' tomorrow evening.

Gerry is just opening the blind as she gets to the end of this.

Staring in at the window is Lydia!! Large as life.

GERRY

Jesus Christ!

He slams down the blind again.

HELEN

What?

GERRY
(*covering madly*)

Jesus Christ that's . . . that's not a 'small' thing. It's huge! It's just great. That's the best news.

Helen goes over to the blind.

HELEN

Is the blind buggered again?

Gerry panicking. Staring.

GERRY

No no . . . er, I . . .

Helen opens the blind again. Gerry cringes as it goes up. He is about to leap into the 'I can explain everything' routine.

There is no one there. He gasps with relief. Helen is back over to the tea.

HELEN

You all right?

GERRY

Yes, yes, I'm just . . . that's great news. I'm thrilled.

The phone rings. Gerry picks it up.

Hello . . . Oh hello, Russ.

INTERCUT WITH:

EXT. GERRY'S FLAT. DAY

Lydia on her mobile phone.

LYDIA

Don't pretend I'm Russell, you know I hate that. I suggest you come and see me. We have things to discuss.

GERRY
(*bluffing*)

Oh, really. What a drag. Yeah, of course, mate, sure. I'll give you a hand. Yeah, yeah, that's fine. Cheers.

INT. GERRY'S FLAT. DAY

Gerry hangs up.

GERRY

Russell's family descending unannounced. Wants me to help him clear his spare room out tomorrow night. Right, I'm off up the library.

He walks out of the room, leaving Helen looking deflated that her wind has been taken away.

Gerry pops his head back round the door.

Sorry, what was the other thing you wanted to tell me?

HELEN

Doesn't matter. It's not important . . .

The door shuts.

. . . evidently.

She looks sad.

Ext. Russell's flat. Early morning

A few days later. Russell opens the door to his flat having just woken up to find Gerry on the doorstep.

Gerry

Nothing!

He pushes past Russell into the flat.

Russell

Hello, Russ, sorry to call round so early without warning only

I'm an ignorant twat.

Russell wearily closes the door.

Int. Russell's flat. Kitchen. Early morning

Small poky kitchen. Russell calmly puts the kettle on as Gerry paces frustratedly.

Gerry
I've tried to check if he has a criminal record or, you know, something, I don't know. Nobody will tell me anything. Not in the public domain or some such cods. His company is all above board and solvent. Nothing there. He's away on business in Newcastle so I can't even snoop on him in a degenerate fashion. There has to be something. There has to be. I can just tell. But I'll get it. Whatever it is. I'm really going off him, I tell you.

Russell is casually making tea. His back to Gerry.

Russell
Have you checked with his wife? Maybe she can help.

Gerry
Russell, just for once, you know! You're a funny bloke but . . .

Russell
He's married, Gerry. He has a wife. My mate at the restaurant told me. I meant to tell you.

Gerry
Are you serious?

Russell
Yes. I definitely meant to tell you. Claudia. Married three years. She runs the homeopathy shop in Camden High Street. Spends all day knocking up cures for cancer out of dandelions and pine kernels. Crap detective, aren't you?

Cut to:

Int. Helen's office. Day

Helen sits at her desk twiddling a pencil. She is preoccupied.

Her work is not getting her attention. Her secretary Rachel is collating a business proposal.

The phone rings. Helen answers hopefully.

> **Helen**
> Hello? Oh, hi, Anna . . . No, he hasn't . . . because I don't think I should, I don't think I want to . . . Alright I do think I want to but I don't think I should . . . OK? I do think I want to but you think I should. Anna you're not helping. Maybe you should phone him – No! I didn't say that. I have to go, I've got lots of work to ignore.

She hangs up. Looks at the phone for a while.

Picks it up. Puts it down. Picks it up again – dials two numbers. Disconnects with her finger. Releases. Looks at the dial. Dials all but one number, thinks and disconnects. She puts down the phone and sits back, staring at it. She is motionless. Deep in thought.

Suddenly she picks up the phone again and dials the full number. Her legs are going like a train under the table.

Int. James's office. Day

James's Secretary answers the phone.

> **James's Secretary**
> Hammerton Enterprises.

Int. Helen's office. Day

Helen puts down the phone quickly as if it is red hot. Her heart pounding. She gets up and walks to the other side of the office.

She snaps herself out of her crazy syndrome and picks up her coat.

Helen

Rachel, I'm going to the shops. Want anything?

Rachel

No thanks. You OK?

Helen

Yeah, yeah I'm fine. See you in a minute.

She leaves the office.

Cut to:

Int. American diner. Day

Helen sits in the American diner playing with a milkshake just as she did when James took her there.

She is deep in thought. She takes a sip. Looks at the milkshake and pushes it away.

She gets up and leaves.

Cut to:

Ext. street near James's office. Day

Helen walks past a phone box. She hesitates, slows down, then keeps walking. She looks up at James's office, deciding what to do. She turns to go and walks right into James. He is with a couple of colleagues.

James doesn't realise it's her immediately.

James

Oh I'm sorr– Helen! Hello.

Helen

Oh, hello.

They are both immediately mortified with embarrassment and panic. They ask and answer simultaneously in a conversational nightmare.

How are you doing? I'm OK. Great, yeah. Er . . . ha ha.

James

How are you? Fine. I'm fine, I'm, how are you? Sorry, you're
great – sorry. Er, guys, I'll catch you up.

The Colleagues walk off. They look at each other.

Helen

Going for lunch?

James

Yes, just, er . . . business lunch, you know.

A tiny nervous moment.

Helen

I thought you were away on business.

James

I was . . . I, er . . . I got back last night as a matter er . . . Helen,
look, please don't think that . . .

Helen

It's OK. I haven't thought – I don't think, I mean I don't think that
– or not . . .

James wants to get this so right he sounds like someone explaining
the principles of space travel for the first time.

James

No, I mean don't think that I . . . that I have 'not called you'. I
haven't 'not called you'. I mean I don't mean that I haven't not
called you 'cos that's a double negative so as to say I have
called you.

Helen

When did you call?

James

I didn't. Er. But I didn't not call you in the way you may think I

didn't call you. Oh dear, look, there um . . . I wanted to call you,
I mean I even did that dial all but the last number thing and then
not, er . . . ridiculous behaviour.

Helen is smiling.

Helen

Totally.

James laughs in a flattered awkward way. This is still polite stuff but
the undercurrent is massive.

A moment.

James

You see, I thought that you had to still deal with your other, er,
the er . . .

Helen

Gerry?

James

I don't know . . . Is that . . . Yes if . . . and I thought it better if I
allowed you to . . .

Helen

Gerry is why you haven't called me?

James

Well, after Clive's party I thought . . . I didn't want to just
presume that you . . . we . . . you know, if he . . .

Helen

You thought I just go to bed with all successful oarsmen I come
across. Sorry – nervous humour.

James

Well, I hoped not.

James's mobile phone rings.

'Scuse me.

(answering)

Hello. I see. No, I'll come straight away.

(to Helen)

My mum had to go into hospital. She had some tests done and the results are through. I have to go. I'm sorry.

Helen

Do you want me to come with you?

James

Well, yeah that's really nice of you – ah, well, maybe it's . . . She's quite frail. You know . . . I don't know how she'll be and . . .

Helen

OK.

James

But thanks. Helen, it's so good to see you. I'll er . . . look, maybe we could, um, well could I, er, I mean I'll call you if that's OK and we, um, we can, er . . . you know . . . maybe.

Helen

Is that a 'will' call me or a 'haven't not didn't might'?

He smiles. They hug each other in a 'friendly manner'.

Don't worry about your mum. She'll be OK. Remember Monty Python.

They separate. He hails a cab, gets in and waves at her as it pulls off.

Cut to:

Ext. hospital. Day

James waits outside the entrance. Claudia arrives in a taxi and gets out.

They embrace each other and go in to the hospital.

INT. GERRY'S FLAT. LIVING ROOM. EVENING

Helen sits with Anna.

> ANNA
> Is Gerry excited about being a daddy?

> HELEN
> I haven't told him yet. Never seems to be the right moment, somehow.

> ANNA
> Ooh, let's celebrate. What have you got?

Helen looks around the room. Sees a couple of bottles of booze.

> HELEN
> Brandy?

> ANNA
> Ooh no, yuk. Makes me vomit.

> HELEN
> Advocaat?

> ANNA
> Yerrr! Go on then.

Helen pours two glasses of advocaat.

INT. BERTORELLI'S. NIGHT

Helen, deep in thought, is clearing away some glasses from a table. One of them is a brandy glass. She looks at it momentarily, curious.

Int. Anna's living room. Night

Anna sits at her desk doing some sketching. Helen comes in, in a nice outfit. She stands at the door and looks at Anna for approval. Anna gives an approving face. Helen leaves.

Clive's restaurant. Night

Through the window. James and Helen sit with 3 of Clive's mates –
they are eating, chatting, laughing etc.

As we move in James and Helen look casually at each other. As they
do their eyes and hearts lock simultaneously and the rest of the
world disappears. They simply stare at each other along the fervent
line of passion that suddenly consumes them.

Ext. street outside Anna's house. Night

Helen and James walk up the road side by side. They look dead
ahead. No dialogue. There is an incredible 'tension' of inevitability
about them that defies the need for words. An intense knowledge of
what is happening.

Int. Anna's kitchen. Night

Empty frame – James and Helen's faces come in from left and right.
They stare at each other for a second. Then their lips meet in a light,
loving sensuous kiss – they pull back and stare at each other again –
their lips come together again.

Int. Helen's office. Day

Helen is checking her diary for appointments. She stops, noticing a
circled cross three days earlier in the week. She flicks back four
weeks to the last circled cross. It has a tick by it. Back to the latest
circled cross. She looks into space.

> Cut to:

Ext. Claudia's homeopathy shop. Day

Gerry and Russell stand over the road from the shop. Claudia arrives
and opens the shop with a key. Gerry takes photos.

Russell looks at him.

Gerry

Just practising.

Int. Anna's flat. Living room. Day

Anna is sitting on the floor in some new fangled yoga position watching TV. Helen walks in in a strange trance-like way.

Anna

Half day?

Helen hands a predictor test to Anna. She looks at it.

James?

Helen nods.

Sorry. You can't tell from one. They can be inaccurate.

Helen

I bought three packets. Two in a packet. That's six. You can tell from six.

Anna

What are you going to do?

Ext. Claudia's homeopathy shop. Day

Claudia gets into a taxi outside her shop. Gerry and Russell get into their car and follow her.

Int. James's office. Day

Helen arrives in reception. The secretary greets her.

Helen

Hello, is James Hammerton in?

Receptionist

No, I'm afraid not.

Helen

Do you know when he's due back?

Receptionist

I'm not sure. He's gone to visit his mother in hospital with his wife. Would you like to leave a message?

Helen stares. Her voice becomes faint.

Helen

What?!

Receptionist

Can I take a name and number? I'll get him to call you.

Helen

Er . . . no . . . Thank you.

She sidles out of the office and gets to the door and almost faints against the exit sliding doors. Her face is a blank of confusion and destruction. She is standing on the pressure mat and the sliding doors open and shut – open and shut – open and shut repeatedly as she stands staring blankly into space.

Ext. Hospital. Day

Claudia and James emerge from the exit. They stand and talk closely. She hugs him. The sound of a camera whipping off shots.

Gerry and Russell stand behind a bush snapping away. Russell is generally disinterested. Gerry's gaze wanders and falls upon Helen getting out of a taxi and standing staring at the couple. Russell doesn't see this.

Gerry sees Helen who looks at James and Claudia for a few seconds. He sees her crushed look. Helen gets back in the taxi and it zooms off. Gerry suddenly looks very vulnerable and lost.

Gerry

I must be sick in the head. Come on. I'm not doing this.

Russell

Oh, fair enough. Just as well. I was starting to feel guilty about how much fun I was having.

Gerry hasn't heard. He walks away, head down.

INT. GERRY'S FLAT. LIVING ROOM. EVENING

Gerry is typing. Helen comes in and stands staring at him.

HELEN

There's something I want you to know.

He looks at her. She steels herself.

Anna doesn't drink brandy, Gerry, it makes her vomit. And those glasses were not used at the party. They only come out for special dinners. You know that.

GERRY

Am I meant to immediately get the reference here?

HELEN

Are you having an affair, Gerry? Just tell me yes or no. Straight answer.

GERRY

Oh, I see. No. I'm not. I categorically am not. Is that what these last few days have been about? No. Straight answer. I'm not seeing anyone else.

He goes to her and holds her shoulders tenderly. He looks deep into her eyes. He talks gently.

Look in my eyes, Helen. I am not having an affair. OK? I'm not. I don't know about the glass. Really.

Helen just looks at him.

HELEN

Well, look, I shouldn't have brought this up now, I've got to

go to my interview. We'll talk later. Are you going to be in when I get back?

GERRY

Yes. Of course.

She nods to confirm that this is a firm date for a meeting. She picks up her coat and goes to the door.

Helen.

She turns to him. He isn't sure what to say.

Listen, good luck, OK?

She nods thank you and leaves.

Gerry looks at his watch, grabs his coat and leaves the flat.

Int. Anna's flat. Evening

Telephone rings. Anna answers.

Anna

Hello.

Her face sets.

Intercut with next scene.

Ext. street. Evening

James

Hi Anna, is Helen there?

Anna
(*voice-over*)

You've got a damned nerve phoning here.

James

What?

But Anna has hung up.

Cut to:

Int./Ext. Anna's flat. Evening

James stands on the outside of the front door. The door is shut.

James
Anna, please just open the door. I don't know what's going on.

Anna opens the door with the chain lock on. There is a three-inch gap through which James attempts to get into the flat.

Anna
You don't know what's going on? I'll tell you, then. She saw you, James. At the hospital. With your wife. You know, the one with the wedding ring. What is it with you bloody men? We're not just . . .

James
Oh, Jesus. Anna, let me in. This is a mistake.

Anna
You're telling me!

James
Anna, please let me see her, I can . . .

Anna
She's not here.

James
Where is she?

Anna
What's it to you? I don't know.

She shuts the door in his face. He is left standing on the doorstep. James walks agitatedly back and forth on the spot.

James
Shit, shit, bollocks. Oh God, you idiot!

Quick montage sequence:

Int. Bertorelli's. Evening

The door bursts open and James comes in. He looks around the bar.
It is fairly empty. Helen is not there.

Cut to:

Int. Clive's restaurant. Night

James running along the road. He arrives at Clive's restaurant. He
bursts in. Clive is discussing a menu with one of his staff.

James

Have you seen Helen?

Clive

No. Why, is . . .

But James is gone.

Cut to:

Ext. Albert Bridge. Evening

Close shot: of Helen's face staring. Unanimated. We are not sure
where she is from this shot.

Ext. street outside Helen's office. Evening

James is standing outside Helen's office. He is on the mobile phone.
He hears the phone 'answered'.

Int. Helen's office. Evening

The room is dark. Uninhabited. The answermachine clicks on.

Cut to:

Ext. American diner. Night

James runs in to the diner. He looks left and right. It is empty.

James's face as he realises she is not there. He is hot and sweaty now. Red-faced. Out of breath.

He leaves the diner and stands, leaning against the window, hands on his knees, looking down. He looks up, trying to think of where else he can look. A tiny look of realisation comes across his face. He heads off again.

Ext. Albert Bridge. Night

Helen stands alone looking over the water. She is still in a dazed state. It has started to rain lightly.

James arrives at speed on to the other end of the bridge. He looks around searching for Helen but he can't see her through the rain in the dark.

He is frantic. This is the last place he could think of where she might be.

Helen suddenly comes into view as she starts to walk away at the other end of the bridge. James sets after her at a pace.

James

Helen! Helen, wait.

She keeps on walking, ignoring him.

He arrives out of breath. Helen keeps walking. He keeps up with her as she stares ahead.

Helen. Helen, you've made a mistake. I, oh, Jesus, I'm such an idiot. Look at me, please.

She just keeps on walking. He stops her and pulls her round to him. She stares at him, unmoved. He grabs her shoulders.

128

Helen

Let go of me. Let me go.

James

Helen, listen . . .

She spins on him in anger.

Helen

No, you listen. I never want to see you again. OK? I have been through enough for one year. I stupidly believed that here was a man who was different from 'men'. But it's clear I made a mistake. You are all of you varying shapes and sizes of the same prick! Now do me a favour and go away!

She walks off. He looks after her. After a moment.

James

I am married, Helen. But I'm separated. Walk away if you want but take this with you. The woman you saw today was the woman I married three years ago . . .

Helen's face. She has slowed down. She wants to keep going but her legs won't go at the speed she wants them to. They are about thirty yards apart.

She left me six months ago and soon we will be divorced. Nothing aggressive. She just realised she didn't want to be married and I had to let her go. It happens. And I'll be honest, it hurt me because I loved her and at the time I begged her to stay. My mother is ill in hospital as you know and Claudia agreed to keep up the pretence that we were OK still. For my mum. It was a favour. That's all. She is a very decent woman. Do you have a mum, Helen . . . ?

Helen has stopped. She turns to look at him. The drizzle is stronger.

James is very focused and precise.

Helen. If we're not going to be together then let's make sure it's for the right reason. And just now there is no reason. None.

There is just confusion. And it can be erased in a split second. I don't want my ex-wife back. I haven't since the day I met you. I want you back. I didn't tell you before bec– I don't know why I . . . I have wanted to tell you so many times but it . . . er . . .I didn't want to presume that . . . and now you've found out a 'different' way. I wish I'd told you before, but . . .

Helen
Well, where is retrospect when you really need it? James, is this the truth? If it's not, then you just have to . . .

He starts to walk slowly towards her. He is getting something out of his pocket. It is a small box.

James
This is almost certainly the worst segue in the history of romance but . . . I bought you something.

He stops ten feet away and holds it up. A long moment.

Helen
A box.

James
Yeah, well, you know – I was going to buy you a book, but Anna tells me you've already got one.

They look deeply at each other. She walks slowly back to him. Their faces are now close.

Permission to engage the enemy, sir?

She looks at him deeply for several seconds. Makes a life decision. She speaks softly.

Helen
Granted.

He leans forward and kisses her gently. Wide as they fall into each others arms.

Cut to:

INT./EXT. LYDIA'S FLAT. NIGHT

Lydia opens the door. It is Gerry. She opens the door for him to come in. He is aggressive. Out of breath.

> GERRY
> Ten minutes, Lydia. And don't you ever turn up at my flat again like that. Understand? It's over, you know. You said it yourself.

She is calm.

> LYDIA
> I know. Sorry. I wasn't thinking. I just want to show you something.

CUT TO:

Gerry sits on the sofa. He is holding a positive predictor test in his hand.

> LYDIA
> I could deal with it myself, sure. But you know what, why should I? I'm feeling just a mite 'woman scorned' and it's making me act a little cookie, you know. I have to go to the bathroom. You sit there and look dazed for a moment.

She goes into her bedroom off the living room. Gerry just sits and looks at the test slide.

CUT TO:

Lydia in the bathroom looking in the mirror. Doing nothing.

EXT. LYDIA'S APARTMENT COMPLEX. NIGHT

Helen walks along checking with her directions, trying to find the right block of flats.

INT. LYDIA'S FLAT. NIGHT

Gerry paces up and down looking at the test slide.

Inside the bathroom Lydia sits on the edge of the bath.

The door bell goes. She looks at her watch and then calls.

>LYDIA
>Get that, would you?

In the living room Gerry goes to the front door. He opens it.

It is Helen!!

She stares in at him, completely dumbfounded, and he at her. They are both momentarily speechless.

The moment is broken.

>(*voice-over*)
>Of course, if you don't want it, darling, I can always lose it.

She opens the sliding doors to the hall. She is now wearing a red negligée with a glass of champagne in her hand.

>LYDIA
>Who is it? Oh. Hello again. So glad you could come. You're right on time. Thing is, I can't take the interview just now – I'm discussing whether or not I'm going to keep your boyfriend's baby. I'm sorry you had to hear it this way.

Helen's face, Gerry's face, Helen looks at Lydia.

Everything flashes through Helen's mind at once. The glass – the noise in the hotel. His flowers.

We bang in closer and closer to Helen as the whole realisation envelopes her and she suddenly runs away from the door.

EXT. CORRIDOR/STAIRWAY OUTSIDE LYDIA'S. NIGHT

Gerry chases after Helen screaming at her to stop. Helen bursts through the door to the staircase. Gerry grabs her arm. She is very violent in her attempts to free herself.

Helen, please, stop, wait. I can . . .

HELEN

GET OFF ME!!! LET GO OF ME!!!!

She rips herself free of him with great violence and the momentum takes away her footing and she falls headlong down the concrete staircase knocking herself unconscious.

CUT TO:

Ext. London Road. Night

Helen and James walk along arm in arm. They are silent. Helen stops and stands in front of him. Holds his collar.

Helen

James, there's something I have to tell you.

James

What?

Helen sees a phone box across the street.

Helen

Oh, look I really should phone Anna to tell her I'm OK.

James

Mind if I stay here? She scares me. What do you want to tell me?

Helen

Wait there. I'll tell you in a minute. See if you can find somewhere to sit down.

She kisses him deeply. Stares deeply and lovingly into his eyes.

Helen walks out into the road. He calls to her.

James

Helen.

She turns back in the middle of the road.

I love you.

Helen

Find a seat.

She turns round to keep walking as a van comes round the corner at speed and smashes straight into her.

James

HELEN!!!!

Ext. London Roads. Night

An ambulance screeches along the road – sirens blazing.

EXT. LONDON ROADS. NIGHT

Another ambulance blazes along from the opposite direction to ambulance in the previous scene.

Int. hospital corridor. Night

Helen is being rushed on a stretcher by the crash team to the theatre. She is still in a lot of pain and close to unconsciousness. James urgently brings up the rear.

Mix to:

INT. HOSPITAL CORRIDOR. NIGHT

Helen is being rushed down the corridor. She is unconscious. She has a big bandage round her head where her wound has been treated in the ambulance. Gerry urgently brings up the rear.

CUT TO:

Int. theatre. Night

The mayhem that surrounds a now unconscious Helen, with drips and monitors all in action. Two theatre Nurses attend the Surgeon who frantically tries to save Helen.

The Surgeon talks to a Theatre Nurse. She leaves the room.

Int. hospital corridor. Night

James stands a little way away. He is beside himself with grief. A Senior Theatre Nurse comes over to him.

> **Nurse**
> James. Are you her husband?

> **James**
> I'm . . . I will be. We're getting married.

> **Nurse**
> Helen has suffered major internal injuries, James. She has lost her baby, I'm afraid. You did know she was pregnant?

His face. Marbelized with shock.

> **James**
> Oh. Er . . . she'll be OK, won't she?

The Nurse's face shows that she can't guarantee that.

> Mix to:

INT. HELEN'S INTENSIVE CARE ROOM. NIGHT

A Nurse faces Gerry. In the background Helen lies unconscious with drips coming out of her.

> **NURSE**
> I'm afraid Helen has lost her baby. Did you know she was pregnant?

Gerry's stunned face.

> **GERRY**
> Oh. She . . . she's going to wake up though, isn't she?

The Nurse can't guarantee anything.

NURSE
Would you like me to bring you some tea?

INTERCUT NEXT SEQUENCE WITH A SERIES OF MIXES BETWEEN:

Int. hospital theatre. Night

Helen lies on the operating table. Her monitor bleeps away. James looks on and paces urgently. He looks pale and dishevelled.

The Doctors are reaching the point where there is not much more they can do.

INT. HELEN'S INTENSIVE CARE ROOM. NIGHT

Gerry paces up and down as Helen lies unconscious in the bed.

Her monitor bleeps away.

THE URGENCY BUILDS BETWEEN BOTH SCENARIOS. SHOTS OF MONITORS GET CLOSER AND CLOSER UNTIL:

Int. hospital theatre. Night

Close shot: of Helen. The sound of the monitor beeping. Move across to the monitor. James sits by the side of her holding her hand.

James
Helen, for some reason I know you can hear me, and I'm glad we got things sorted out tonight. I'm glad you caught the train that day, I am going to make you so happy. I promise.

He kisses her cheek gently.

The monitor goes to flatline. Continual sound. Helen is dead.

Mix to:

INT. HELEN'S INTENSIVE CARE ROOM. NIGHT

Helen's eyes open. Gerry's face.

He looks down on the conscious Helen.

MIX TO:

INT. HOSPITAL CORRIDOR. MORNING

James Hammerton, whom we have seldom seen in this storyline, walks along the corridor. He wears a *different* outfit from James's and is clean-shaven.

A large Indian family have arrived. Uncles, aunties, grandparents, sisters, cousins, etc. Fifteen of them. They all seem really happy as they get back into the lift muttering about 'not this floor, the next one up', etc.

James is met by the Consultant.

                    JAMES
I'm sorry I'm a little late.

                    CONSULTANT
No problem. I'm pleased to say there is a little improvement in your mother this morning. She is sitting up and she had a full breakfast.

                    JAMES
Oh, that's great.

As they walk off together they pass the small room in which Helen is recovering. We let them go and close in on the room.

INT. HELEN'S INTENSIVE CARE ROOM. HOSPITAL. DAY

Helen removes her hand from Gerry's, who is struggling to explain himself to a now conscious but slightly woozy Helen.

                    GERRY
Helen, I swear it was nothing. It . . . I . . . it was over.

138

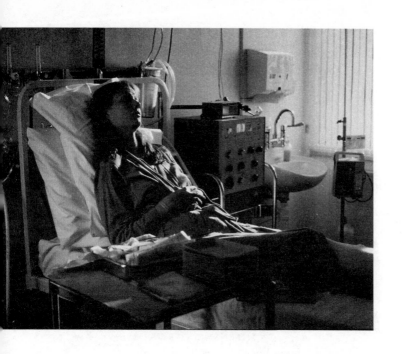

HELEN

Two blows to the head and one to the heart. That's three strikes. You like baseball, Gerry. You know what that means.

He clearly has no line of defence.

GERRY

I'll do anything you want, Helen.

HELEN

Will you? In that case, I want you to stand up, walk over to the door, open it, walk through it, and close it behind you.

His face. He knows she means it. There will be no absolution.

MIX TO:

INT. HELEN'S INTENSIVE CARE ROOM. DAY

Helen, dressed, is leaving. She looks much healthier.

INTENSIVE CARE NURSE

Call us if you have any problems at all.

HELEN

Yes, thanks.

INTENSIVE CARE NURSE

You are very fortunate, Helen. You had a lucky escape.

HELEN

Say that again. Thank you.

INT. HOSPITAL. CORRIDOR. DAY

A door with 'Mrs Mary Hammerton' on it closes and James walks off down the corridor.

A shot of the hospital lift at the end of the corridor.

INT. HOSPITAL. CORRIDOR. DAY

Helen comes out of her room and heads towards the lift.

GO TO SLOW MOTION – INTERCUT BETWEEN JAMES AND
HELEN:

James approaches the lift. Helen approaches the lift.

James arrives, presses the lift call button.

The lift doors open. Inside are the large Indian family now with a
new mother with baby in arms. They take up practically the whole
lift. James gestures 'Go ahead' and lets the doors slide shut.

Helen walks towards the lift.

The next lift arrives and the doors open. It is empty.

Helen sees the doors have opened and walks more quickly.

James steps into the hospital lift. He presses a button. The lift
doors start to close in front of his face.

Helen moves faster towards the lift but she gets there just too late
and the lift doors shut. Helen stands by the lift.

NORMAL SPEED: the lift doors open again. James has his finger on
the open door button.

> JAMES
> I just saw you. Going down?

Helen nods absent-mindedly. She gets in, putting on her earrings.
She drops one on the floor. James picks it up and gives it to her.
She takes it without looking at him.

> HELEN
> (*miles away*)
> Thanks.

> JAMES
> Cheer up. You know what the Monty Python boys say.

And with no pause *whatsoever*, as if she is not in control of what she is saying.

HELEN

Nobody expects the Spanish Inquisition.

She immediately looks at him: 'How did I know to say that?' He is staring at her: 'I don't know.'

And as 'James' and 'Helen' look at each other for the 'first time' . . . the sliding doors of the lift gently close.

CLOSING CREDITS

Afterword

You may have noticed from reading the screenplay that, as with most movies, it differs here and there – scenes and dialogue added or taken away etc. – from the actual film.

During the production process those things are inevitable.

However, for me the most interesting differences are things that happened in the editing process with John Smith.

John constantly encouraged me to re-examine the interlacing of the two stories.

You will notice that some scenes written in isolation from each other are cut together. For example Lydia's revelation of her pregnancy to Helen is more intricately cut with the scene of James and Helen on the rainy bridge than in the script. This created a more intriguing cinematic sequence.

This experience taught me a great deal and made me realize that whoever said 'You write a script – You shoot it – Then you go into the editing room and *re-write* it' was right.

Peter Howitt
May 1998

Credits

147

FILM-MAKERS

Written and Directed by	PETER HOWITT
Produced by	SYDNEY POLLACK
	PHILIPPA BRAITHWAITE
	WILLIAM HORBERG
Executive Producers	GUY EAST
	NIGEL SINCLAIR
Director of Photography	REMI ADEFARASIN, BSC
Production Designer	MARIA DJURKOVIC
Music by	DAVID HIRSCHFELDER
Film Editor	JOHN SMITH
Costume Designer	JILL TAYLOR
Casting by	MICHELLE GUISH
Co-Producer	DAVID WISNIEVITZ
Associate Producer	SANDY POUSTIE
Line Producer	HELEN BOOTH
First Assistant Director	RICHARD WHELAN
Second Assistant Director	SARA DESMOND
Third Assistant Director	EMMA GRIFFITHS
Location Manager	MATT STEINMANN
Dialogue Coach	BARBARA BERKERY
Art Director	MARTYN JOHN
Standby Art Director	TATIANA LUND
Property Buyer	JUDY DUCKER
Property Master	BRUCE BIGG
Camera Operator	ALF TRAMONTIN
Focus Puller	JULIAN BUCKNALL
Second Focus Puller	JAY JAY ODEDRA
Clapper Loader	JAMES BLOOM
Second Clapper Loader	CAMILLE GRIFFIN
Sound Mixer	JOHN MIDGLEY
Boom Operator	JUNE PRINZ
Sound Trainee	CRAIG BURNS
Stunt Coordinator	HELEN CALDWELL
Script Supervisor	CERI EVANS COOPER
Gaffer	JIM WILLSON
Best Boys	BARRIE MORE
	MITCH SPOONER
Electricians	IAN FRANKLYN

	MATTHEW DOWLER
Key Grip	JOHN ARNOLD
Key Make-Up Designer	TINA EARNSHAW
Make-Up Artists	REBECCA LAFFORD
	LISA MCDEVITT
Key Hair Dresser	SIMON THOMPSON
Hairstylists	GRAHAM POWNALL
	ZOE TAHIR
Costume Assistant	JANE HAMNETT
Costumer	CHARLOTTE SEWELL
Post Production Supervisor	STEPHEN BARKER
First Assistant Film Editor	JOANNA NODWELL
Second Assistant Film Editor	ADAM BARTON
Digital Sound Editing	PARAMOUNT PICTURES
Dialogue/ADR Editor	LAURA LOVEJOY
Supervising Foley Editor	THOMAS SMALL
Foley Editor	TAMMY FEARING
Sound Editors	DAVID B. COHEN, M.P.S.E.
	BETH STERNER
Foley Artists	SARAH MONAT
	ROBIN HARLAN
Foley Mixer	RANDY K. SINGER
Foley Recordists	CAROLYN SAUER
Assistant Sound Editor	ROBERT MORRISEY
Foley Facilities	PARAMOUNT PICTURES
Re-recording Mixer	CHRIS JENKINS
Re-recording AT	TODD AO HOLLYWOOD
Orchestrations by	DAVID HIRSCHFELDER
	RICKY EDWARDS
Orchestra – Australia	FILM HARMONIX
Music Notation	SAM SCHWARZ
Scoring Mixer	CHRIS SCALLAN
Recording Engineer	CHRIS SCALLAN
Original Music Recorded at	ALDELPHIA STUDIOS
	MELBOURNE AUSTRALIA
Music Editor	JOHN FINKLEA
Assistant Music Editor	SIENNA FINKLEA
Music Coordinator	KAYLIN FRANK
Production Coordinator	ROS DAVIDSON

Assistant Production Coordinator	LAURA EVANS
Production Accountant	JOHN BEHARRELL
Assistant Production Accountant	PENELOPE BEHARRELL
Script Consultant	DOUGLAS MCFERRAN
Production Secretaries	SUZIE SHEARER
	CLAIRE PARISH
Legal Clearances	RUTH HALLIDAY
Assistant to Sydney Pollack	DONNA OSTROFF
Assistant to Philippa Braithwaite	STUART CARTER LAMBERT
Assistant to William Horberg	STEPHANIE COMER
Assistant to Gwyneth Paltrow	SOPHIE LOUDOUN SHAND
Production Runner	MAX GLICKMAN
Floor Runner	ALEX OAKLEY
Art Dept Assistant	LILIANA CIFONELLI
Art Dept Runner	LAURA DISHINGTON
Costume Trainee	ROBERT GREEN
Unit Publicist	ANYA NOAKES
Publicist	MCDONALD & RUTTER
Stills Photographer	ALEX BAILEY
Storyboard Artist	DOUGLAS INGRAM
Casting Assistant	JULIA GALE
Special Effects Supervisor	BOB HOLLOW
Unit Manager	ANDY RICHARDS
Assistant Location Manager	WINK MORDAUNT
Standby Props	WARREN STICKLEY
	MITCH NICLAS
Standby Painter	JIM DYSON
Standby Carpenter	LEE HOSKEN
Standby Riggers	BILL RICHARDS
	MARK RICHARDS
Standby Transport	BILL NIXON
Stage Hands	ALAN CLIFFORD
	SIMON ROBILLIARD
Dressing Props	TED STICKLEY
	PETER BIGG
Props Storeman	RAY ROSE

Construction Manager	MICHAEL BOLEYN
Unit Nurse	JORDAN ARCHER
Driver Coordinator	CHAS NEWENS
Driver to Ms Paltrow	JIM MAGILL
Unit Drivers	TERRY ENGLISH
	DAVID BARRY
	GERRY FLOYD
Minibus Drivers	RAY CHAMBERS
	JAY NICOL
Security	TONY DENHAM
Caterers	SET MEALS

SOUNDTRACK ALBUM
AVAILABLE ON JERSEY/MCA CD'S AND CASSETTES

'HAVE FUN, GO MAD'
Written by Blair Mackichan/Phil Taylor
Performed by Blair
Courtesy of Mercury Records, Ltd

'HONKY CAT'
Written by Elton John & Bernie Taupin
Performed by Elton John
Courtesy of Polygram Records

'BENNIE AND THE JETS'
Written by Elton John & Bernie Taupin
Performed by Elton John
Courtesy of Polygram Records

'AMATEUR'
Written by Aimee Mann & Jon Brion
Performed by Aimee Mann
Courtesy of Geffen Records

'CALL ME A FOOL'
'GOT A THING ABOUT YOU'
Written by Andre Barreau
Performed by Those Magnificent Men
Courtesy of Those Magnificent Men

'TURN BACK TIME'
Written by Soren Rastad, Claus Norreen, J Pederson & Delgado
Performed by Aqua
Courtesy of MCA Records

'GOOD ENOUGH'
Written by Nigel Clark, Andrew Miller & Matthew Priest
Performed by Dodgy
Courtesy of A&M UK

'USE THE FORCE'
Written by Jay Kay, Toby Smith, McKenzie & Akingbola
Performed by Jamiroquai
Courtesy of Work Records

'MORE LOVE'
Written by Siedah Garrett & Simon Bartholomew
Performed by Brand New Heavies
Courtesy of Delicious Vinyl, Inc.

'TENDERNESS ON THE BLOCK'
Written by Warren Zevon & Jackson Browne
Performed by Patty Larkin
Courtesy of Columbia Records

'ON MY OWN'
Written by Pascal Gabriel, Lisa Lamb & Paul Statham
Performed by Peach Union
Courtesy of Mute/Epic Records

'DON'T FEEL LIKE CRYIN''
Written by Abre Moore
Performed by Abra Moore
Courtesy of Arista Records, Inc.

'DRUG SOUP'
Written by Richard McNiven-Duff
Performed by Space Monkeys
Courtesy of Interscope

'MIRACLE'
Written by Tim Kellett & Robin Taylor-Firth
Performed by Olive
Courtesy of RCA Records

'COMING UP FOR AIR'
Written by Patty Larkin
Performed by Patty Larkin
Courtesy of Windham Hill Group

'THANK YOU'
Written by Dido Armstrong & Paul Herman
Performed by Dido
Courtesy of Arista Records, Inc.

WITH SPECIAL THANKS TO:

Freda Angus, Chris Ball, Simon Chalkley, Jill Cohen,
Clifford Davis, Harlan Goodman, Steve Harding,
Tim Johnson, Kevin Koloff, Sue Latimer, John Ptak,
Marissa Roman, Joan Stigliano, Will Tyrer,
The Whitehouse, London

THE FULL MONTY

Simon Beaufoy

The Full Monty opened in the summer of 1997 and by the spring of 1998 had become the most successful UK box-office release of all time.

This heart-warming and hilarious screenplay contains the complete shooting script to the film which includes a number of scenes that didn't make it to the finished movie.

Illustrated throughout with stills from the film.

ISBN 1 901680 02 9

Paperback, 162pp

£7.99

NIL BY MOUTH

Gary Oldman

A tough, raw utterly convincing portrait of those on the edge of society. The screenplay contains an extensive introduction by the film's producer, together with over 20 full page photographs.

ISBN 1 901680 03 7

Paperback 160pp

£8.99

Also available is the photo-diary accompanying the film and containing an extensive selection of photographs taken on set by Jack English, this edition is limited and individually signed and numbered by Gary Oldman.

ISBN 1 901680 04 5

Hardback 96pp

£45.00

TWENTYFOURSEVEN

Paul Fraser and Shane Meadows

Set in the East Midlands, **TwentyFourSeven** shows how Alan Darcy, a small man with a big heart, tries to give himself and the young unemployed lads he knows some purpose in life by forming a boxing club.

Meadows' film is one of the most eagerly awaited debut features or recent times, and writing with Fraser they have provided Hoskins with one of the best roles of his career.

This edition also includes the screenplays for **Where's the Money Ronnie?** and **Left** (Smalltime)

Illustrated throughout with stills from the film

ISBN 1 901680 07 X

Paperback, 160pp

£8.99

LOVE AND DEATH ON LONG ISLAND

Richard Kwietniowski

The hilariously and touching tale of the obsession harboured by reclusive, novelist Giles Dea'th for the hunky but not very talented American pin-up Ronnie Bostock.

Kwietnioswski has written a literate and affectionate 'fish out of water' comedy, which never overplays its *Death in Venice* references.

This, the original screenplay, is illustrated throughout with stills from the film and contains additional scenes that don't appear in the film.

ISBN 1 901680 08 8

Paperback, 148pp

£7.99

TWIN TOWN

Kevin Allen and Paul Durden

Set in contemporary Swansea, Allen and Durden's writing transforms a deeply disturbing tale of revenge into one of the most exuberant black comedies of our time.

ISBN 1 901680 00 2

Paperback 160pp

£8.99

GREAT EXPECTATIONS

Mitch Glazer

This radically reworked version of Dicken's classic novel follows the journey of Finn Bell, an aspiring artist whose world is changed dramatically by three disparate strangers whom unexpectedly invade his life: Lustig, a dangerous convict, the icy and beautiful Estella; and the wealthy and crazed eccentric Miss Dinsmoor.

A tale of universal truths and unrequited love.

ISBN 1 901680 09 6

Paperback, 148pp

£7.99

ONE FINE DAY

Ellen Simon and Terrel Seltzer

When Jack, a hard hitting newspaper columnist and Mel, a career minded architect are inadvertently thrown together for one chaotic day, the only thing they have in common is identical cellular phones. The last thing they need is to get involved with each others lives, jobs and kids.

A beautifully crafted romance for the modern age.

ISBN 1 901680 01 0

Paperback, 96pp

£7.99

All books are available with FREE POST AND PACKING from

THE BOOK SERVICE

01206 256000

When ordering please quote: TFS

AVAILABLE NOW

MUSIC FROM THE MOTION PICTURE INCLUDES THE HIT SINGLE BY
AQUA - TURN BACK TIME

1. **BLAIR** Have Fun Go Mad
2. **SPACE MONKEYS** Drug Soup
3. **AQUA** Turn Back Time
4. **DODGY** Good Enough
5. **DIDO** Thank You
6. **JAMIROQUAI** Use The Force
7. **OLIVE** Miracle
8. **PEACH UNION** On My Own
9. **AIMEE MANN** Amateur
10. **ELTON JOHN** Honky Cat
11. **ABRA MOORE** Don't Feel Like Cryin'
12. **THOSE MAGNIFICENT MEN** Call Me A Fool
13. **BRAND NEW HEAVIES** More Love